THE BETTER WAYS
OF KILLING

The ninja today is undoubtedly a much better empty-hand fighter than his ancestor was. He has been exposed to the many styles that exist in the world today. He is in the position to choose the best of each and can now become a far more formidable and fearsome fighter than ever before.

The medieval ninja certainly knew both grappling and striking techniques, but they were taught and practiced as two separate and distinct styles and were rarely combined. Today, the ninja knows the two can be quite effective when combined. A grab, sweep and punch are far better and much more disabling than just a grab; a punch, sweep and stomp can do much more damage than just a punch. Though the ancient techniques are still very valid, the new additions and refinements make them that much more lethal.

Al Weiss and Tom Philbin

CLAN OF DEATH: NINJA

PUBLISHED BY POCKET BOOKS NEW YORK

Another *Original* publication of POCKET BOOKS

**POCKET BOOKS, a Simon & Schuster division of
GULF & WESTERN CORPORATION
1230 Avenue of the Americas, New York, N.Y. 10020**

ISBN: 0-671-43046-7

First Pocket Books printing April, 1981

10 9 8 7 6 5 4 3 2 1

POCKET and colophon are trademarks of Simon & Schuster.

Printed in the U.S.A.

ACKNOWLEDGMENTS

We'd like to acknowledge the support and cooperation of Master Steve Hayes, American representative of the Togakure Ryu of ninjutsu, and Master Ron Duncan of New York. They gave unselfishly of their time, advice and expertise in the true spirit of bushido.

We'd also like to thank Larry Beaver of Beaver Products for supplying us with photos and ninja equipment used in the preparation of this book.

We owe a debt of gratitude to Chris McLoughlin for allowing us to use his research on Steve Hayes and ninjutsu; to Joe Griffith and Chuck Norris for supplying us with illustrative photos.

Bibliography

CONTENTS

INTRODUCTION

"How many of you here could *not* assassinate someone? Raise your hands," Stephen K. Hayes, a master teacher of the Togakure Ryu system of ninjutsu, asked a group of men assembled for a seminar and demonstration of ninja bare-handed fighting and weapons techniques in Atlanta, Georgia.

Not one hand was raised.

"You mean, every man in this room is capable of assassinating someone?"

There were a few nodded assents, one quiet "yes sir" . . . the others were silent.

"Why would you assassinate someone?" he asked. "What would drive you to such an extreme act?"

He pointed to the man closest to him.

"To protect my family—my wife and children."

He continued pointing at the men in the room, and they called out their answers.

"For a good cause."

"To help a friend or someone close to me."

"To save my country."

"To help the world become a better place."

"For money!"

Hayes stopped at this last answer. "For money?" he asked. "How much money? Five hundred dollars?"

The man leaning on the wall smiled, thought for a moment, then answered. "Hell no. I wouldn't do it for less than five thousand."

The group became silent, thoughtful. The seminar was over.

What we had seen impressed us. What we had heard in those last moments from those who attended from all parts of the country (we have no idea how many of them were truly ninja) was an introduction to the diversity of ninja thought—a microcosm of ninja philosophy. There were, and perhaps are, ninja who would snuff out a life for a small payment, maybe even for pleasure. To men like Steve Hayes, they didn't deserve to call themselves ninja. To him, they were nothing more than criminals in black clothing. They were the mercenaries, the opportunists, the cruel and sadistic. They comprised the segment of ninja society that inspired the legends of "the killers of the night" that we read about and see in films—those insidious phantoms who preyed on the samurai and warlords of feudal Japan, leaving a trail of death and destruction.

But there were also those ninja who believed they had a higher calling. Men and women of strong religious beliefs whose acts, in their eyes, were performed for the benefit of mankind. They served their religion, their family, their friends. Though few in number, they were a strong, independent people whose philosophy made them become absolutely and totally involved in the preservation of their society. They felt personally responsible for every detail of their existence and the existence of those around them. They would not, because of their strong independent natures, allow others to do things for them—or to them. This is one of the main reasons why it was possible for these religious, basically peaceful people to become such aggressive warriors.

But whatever the reasons for their actions—whether or not they acted for personal gain or for the good of the community or mankind—they were, by far, some of the most effective warriors in history. They were the masters of "the art of stealth," students of all facets of the military sciences. They were a resourceful people and could easily adapt to a new, unfamiliar environment, and they were fluid enough in their thinking to accept and respond quickly and decisively to unexpected developments.

As times changed, so did the ninja. He learned to discard the useless and keep those elements of his art that were still valid and practical. He adjusted quickly to new technologies and incorporated into his arsenal of information and weapons those innovations that would improve his performance. The firelock replaced the staff, the machine pistol replaced the firelock.

But one aspect of the ninja's life has never changed: his penchant for secrecy. For this reason, what knowledge we have of him is limited; but with the information available to us through the few recorded histories and interviews with present-day ninja, we have tried to present an accurate picture of this formidable warrior . . . his fighting skills, his world, his reason for being.

The information in this book is presented to introduce the reader to a fascinating and exciting people and the period during which they lived. Our intention is to inform, not to instruct. The techniques and weapons discussed in this book can be dangerous and should not be used except under the supervision of a certified instructor.

Chapter 1

MEET THE NINJA

During feudal times in Japan, the <u>samurai war-</u><u>rior, or *bushi*,</u> held sway. He followed a rigid code of honor, punishable by hara-kiri ("ritual suicide") if violated, and his skills as a fighter, wielding a fearsome *katana* (a long sword), were legendary. On the surface, the average samurai seemed afraid of nothing.

But he was afraid, or at least had a most healthy respect for another kind of warrior: a samurai from the dark side of the moon, the ninja. And it was a fear or respect that was emphatically well deserved.

Until a few years ago, not many people had even heard the word ninja, much less understood it. But a number of occurrences have changed that.

Perhaps most telling was the publication of the novel *The Ninja* by Eric Van Lustbader. This four-hundred-page-plus opus took a long, albeit fictional, look at ninja. The book climbed onto the

New York Times bestseller list and stayed there for four months or so.

Also, martial arts moviemaker Chuck Norris came out with "The Octagon," which featured ninja as his adversaries (the picture got its name from the eight-sided headquarters of the ninja in a remote mountain region). So too, another martial arts champion, Mike Stone, wrote a pilot script for a film featuring a good ninja who comes out of retirement when his family is murdered.

Ninja were featured as the bad guys in a couple of James Bond movies, including "You Only Live Twice" in 1967, and ninja have long been staple fare for the Japanese moviegoers. Martial arts magazines have run stories on ninja in recent years, and ninja were in both the novel *Shōgun* and the television mini-series.

Just what is a ninja? It depends on the period one is talking about, but generally he is a practitioner of the art of ninjutsu (which literally means "the art of stealthy movement"). He is a kind of Japanese espionage agent with great skills in stealth, weapons, martial arts, sabotage, arson and assassination who is so adept at disappearing with such great speed that, except for the remains of his actions, one couldn't be sure he had been "there" at all. In short, the kind of guy you wouldn't want to meet in a dark alley, or even a well-lit one; the kind of guy whose fantastic abilities were the origin for the belief that the ninja had supernatural powers and could actually become invisible at will.

Ninja flourished roughly between the twelfth and sixteenth centuries when Japan was ruled by a class of military dictators who exercised complete authority over the many sections of the island kingdom. The power of the emperor and the Imperial Court quickly disappeared when it was no longer possible for the distant central government to maintain security and order and protect the peasants. The local warlords took control, and a feudal system, similar to the one that existed in Europe, grew in power.

Jealous and suspicious, the warlords were constantly at war with each other in their desperate attempts to gain even greater power and territory or, at least, to hold on to the kingdom they controlled. Their armies could wage wars in the field, but when they needed saboteurs, assassins or spies, they employed the deadly skills of the ninja. These fearsome figures, invariably operating at night and dressed in black, were credited with wreaking much havoc and being responsible for many of the "mysterious" deaths that occurred.

There are numerous examples of warlords, seemingly safe in heavily protected fortresses, who were discovered assassinated, with no one ever having seen the assassin; and for just this reason, it could be assumed it was a ninja.

One of the more striking and gruesome of these was the assassination of a *daimyo* ("territorial ruler") named Fugasiti who lived in the mid–sixteenth century (approximately 1540) in Iga Province. He was particularly alert to an assassination attempt and refused to leave his well-guarded palace unless accompanied by a large number of his samurai. The palace itself was surrounded by a deep, wide moat, the one entrance heavily guarded and all access halls to his rooms heavily protected by samurai. Additionally, there was a samurai constantly at Fugasiti's side, and he even stayed with him during the night. One morning the other guards found the bodyguard dead and Fugasiti lying on his *tatami*, his head resting on his stone pillow, his throat cut from ear to ear.

Exploits such as this, seemingly magical abilities to escape and other aspects of ninjutsu, made the populace think of the ninja as superhuman: a scary specter who could do just about anything, from walking on water to becoming invisible.

They were also, for the most part, regarded as villains. The heroes were the samurai, the noble warriors whose power over the life and death of the average person was so shockingly illustrated in "Shōgun" on TV when one samurai summarily cut off the head of a peasant for not bowing. Ninja were regularly employed by samurai to do those jobs that their warrior code would not permit them to do.

For example, it was against the code of the samurai to infiltrate an enemy's palace in the middle of the night and secretly—and unchivalrously—assassinate him. The samurai's Code of Bushido demanded he live by ethical principles (though some did stray from the path). Rooted in Buddhism, Confucianism and Shintoism, the samurai was expected to be just, courageous, benevolent, truthful, loyal, honorable and sincere. The fear of disgrace, if he didn't follow this code, hung over the head of every samurai. If he didn't act in the proper manner, he was often forced, by others or by his own conscience, to commit *seppuku* (hara-kiri). No such code governed the ninja, so these men in black were hired to accomplish the same end in their own devious way.

Following the unification of Japan in 1608 by the great shogun Ieyasu, the need for ninja, like samurai, decreased. They were soldiers without a war. Ieyasu, who considered wisdom the only virtue, encouraged the samurai to study literature and philosophy and contribute to the arts, and militarism slowly decayed. Over the years—the centuries—the samurai and ninja continued to fade from the scene and, indeed, at one point it was made illegal in Japan to practice ninjutsu.

However, the ninja clans never really disbanded; they simply went underground. They have always been there, though certainly fewer than in the past. During World War II, for example, the Japanese high command had ninja-trained troops deployed to assassinate General Douglas MacArthur if and when the opportunity arose. The confusion they needed to succeed with their mission never occurred, and when they were ready to act, the force surrounding MacArthur was too alert and too strong for them to penetrate.

But the ninja did not fail very often. Information on their specific World War II activities is scant, but according to Ron Duncan, a ninja practitioner living in New York, there were many strange incidents which had a ninjaesque quality: cases that were the result of action beyond that of normal warfare. Instances where, for example, sentries or guards were killed and autopsies were unable to reveal the causes of death; instances where men were killed with weapons other than the standard ones, such as *shuriken* (pointed throwing stars that can be coated with poison); instances where allied commanders had been assassinated although extremely well-guarded.

What turned out to be one of the most chilling incidents was a story making the rounds just after the war that told of an entire platoon of Marines that died mysteriously within a twenty-four-hour period. Symptoms included abdominal pain, diarrhea and bloody urine, and it was at first assumed that amoebic dysentery or some tropical disease was the cause. But a young naval lieutenant doctor didn't think so, and his investigation ultimately revealed the real cause. The drinking water had been spiked with arsenic, 0.5 gram per glassful of water—more than enough to do the job.

Poison has long been a favorite technique of ninja.

In 1948, some ninja switched sides, or at least became employed by the CIA, says Duncan. "In 1948, when the OSS became the CIA, ninja were hired to train the new recruits," he explains. "And as far as I know, there are still ninja in the CIA."

Indeed, operations of a violent nature, if they are occurring, are mostly secret. But there was one that had a worldwide spotlight on it from beginning to end, where ninja, Duncan says, could be seen in action.

The event was the taking, in May 1980, of the Iranian Embassy in London by a group of terrorists who called themselves the Iranian Group of the Martyrs. They demanded independence for the oil-rich Arab area of Khuzestan in Iran and also wanted the Ayatollah Khomeini to release ninety-one prisoners.

On May 6, the gunmen, holed up in the plush embassy in Princess Gate with their nineteen hostages, delivered their ultimatum: they were going to start killing a hostage every half hour until their demands were met.

The government found that the terrorists were indeed serious. Within an hour, two of the hostages were murdered. It was then that the decision was made to assault the embassy and release the hostages by force.

Chosen for the job was the SAS (Special Air Service), a force so secret that its core members are known by very few people. In news pictures of the incident, there are many civilians shown in the assault; but the core members are in black, only their eyes showing through the hoods covering their heads. In short, they were in the uniform of the ninja.

"They are ninja," Duncan says, "absolutely. All the elements of a ninja-style operation were there."

Indeed, the forces made a surprise attack, quickly killed three of the terrorists and left the other two quaking with shock and terror. It was all over in minutes. And the SAS just as quickly faded from the scene.

There is no way of telling just how extensive ninja are around the world today. Just as they did in feudal times, ninja thrive on secrecy. Someone told us that he was in Kyushu two summers ago and went into a room where there were five or six businessmen standing around talking. "It was only later," he says, "that I learned they were all ninja."

Indeed, in the old days ninja even strove to keep the fact that they were ninja from close relatives. Having a lot of people knowing you were a ninja could result in death—your own.

We do know, however, that they exist in Japan, and Duncan says that they are all over the world. "A man does not have to be Japanese to be a ninja," Duncan says. "All he has to do is be a practitioner of ninjutsu."

Unlike during the feudal days, ninja do not live together in well-hidden mountain retreats. They can be in any occupation; the ninja part is their other face. Ron Duncan, for example, is a private investigator and also runs a martial arts *dojo* ("school"). While he has revealed his identity as a ninja, he most certainly says nothing about his activities except to say that he had "been approached by some governments" to train people in assassination. He stresses that he himself has never directly killed anyone.

One gets a sense of violence being at the core of the ninja, but Duncan would deny this. "A ninja is many different things," he would say. "It is a spiritual and philosophical approach to life as well as a physical one."

Nobody would probably agree more with that statement than Steve Hayes, a thirty-two-year-old man who says he is the only American-born ninja authorized to teach Japanese ninjutsu.

In the early seventies Hayes traveled to Japan and trained under Dr. Masaaki Hatsumi, of Noda City, Japan, a thirty-fourth-generation ninja of the Togakure Ryu, a ninjutsu style founded in approximately 1550 in the Iga Province near Kyoto, which was the capital of Japan then. Hayes is the only American ever accepted as a personal student by Hatsumi and the only one permitted to establish and promote the Togakure style in this country.

A handsome, articulate man who has done much film work (at this writing his most recent credit is "Shōgun"), Hayes had been studying karate for years, but tired of it. He was looking for something more, and after reading a series of articles on ninjutsu in a martial arts magazine, he became enamored of the incredible art. "It is," he says, "an integration of mind and body." Unlike many martial arts which emphasize only physical aspects, ninjutsu involves the entire man. Hayes is very much opposed to an image of ninja—today or yesterday—as one of a cult of criminals. The fact seems to be that some ninja are bad, some good, some violent, some not violent. But overall, as you will see, they are well deserving of that much overused adjective—incredible.

Chapter 2

HISTORY: BORN IN PEACE, BRED IN BLOOD

The roots of the ninja are as difficult to trace and follow as the footsteps of a ninja warrior in action. Few records were kept; few histories were compiled. What little documentation that exists was assembled, more often than not, by outsiders who bolstered a meager amount of historical fact with a great deal of assumption and myth. The ninja themselves revealed little. They jealously guarded their secrets. Secrecy and anonymity were essential if they were to succeed in their operations . . . and secrecy and anonymity were essential if they wanted to remain alive.

Some ninja leaders received great notoriety. Their feats were so fantastic, they quickly became the subjects of legends. But the vast majority of ninja were never known; their stories were never told, their backgrounds were never revealed. We have general knowledge of the large clans and houses, but the individual ninja remains, for the most part, in the shadows.

What history we know has been collected from many sources, some of them contradictory, from ninja many generations removed from their warrior ancestors, and from a study of the times during which the ninja flourished. To know the ninja and why they existed we must know ancient and feudal Japan.

Ninjutsu ("the art of stealth") was introduced to Japan soon after Buddhism was brought from China and Korea in 522 A.D. The new religion quickly spread through the islands because Shintoism, which did not provide a doctrine of immortality and heaven, did not fully satisfy the religious needs of the people.

When Buddhism was introduced to the Yamato court about 552, Chinese learning gained a strong and permanent foothold in Japan, and Japanese converts traveled to China to learn more about this new religion. When these Japanese student priests returned, they not only brought home a deeper understanding of Buddhism, but also a greater knowledge of Chinese culture . . . its arts, institutions and ideas. We can assume that some of this information concerned military science, including spying and subterfuge—arts with which the Chinese were very familiar.

It was through this introduction of Chinese religion and culture that ninjutsu was born and nourished.

In 586, when the Emperor Yomei died, there was a battle for the succession to the throne that was won by Prince Shotoku Taishi, a Buddhist who established himself as Prince Imperial and Regent (the throne itself was actually occupied by Empress Suiko; until the middle of the eighth century, women occasionally occupied the throne because they were considered socially and politically superior to men). For the twenty-nine years that he ruled (592–621), Shotoku promulgated Buddhism and the arts and culture of China. Though there was peace during this period, Shotoku found it necessary at times to use spies and agents. The "art of stealth" began to develop because of this need for information by the ruling classes and through the efforts of mountain priests who had become adherents of ninjutsu. The priests recognized that their very lives depended on the sufferance of the powerful warlords whose territories they inhabited or bordered on. Few in number, they could not afford to offend those who were capable of overpowering them with masses, if not with ability. So they formed a tacit alliance with their neighbors, offering their knowledge of the Chinese teachings of spying and subterfuge in exchange for security.

These priests, though warriors, were not a violent people. They were mystics, who would later become followers of the "secret knowledge" known as Mikkyo. Ninjutsu (the art) was being studied and taught, but the ninja—as families or clans as we know them from the legends—still did not exist.

Soon after Shotoku's death, a struggle for supremacy between Buddhists and Shintoists began in the court. The mountain priests became involved in these religious conflicts in their attempt to find a solution. To the nobles, they suddenly loomed as a threat, and they found themselves under attack. Greatly outnumbered, these warrior priests were able to survive by making full use of their knowledge of Chinese military sciences.

About a generation after the death of Shotoku, in 645, a palace coup took place, supported by students who had studied in China and led by a lord named Kamatori. The heir apparent was assassinated, and a senile puppet was placed on the throne. The new heir apparent was Prince Naka, later to become Emperor Tenchi. The government was quickly changed from a loose association of autonomous clans into an imperial state, with the emperor the supreme ruler, the "Son of Heaven."

This new, comparatively powerful central government declared that all lands belonged to the emperor, and all areas would be controlled by governors appointed by him. Independent action or attitudes would not be accepted and would be squashed by force. The independent and rebellious *yamabushi* ("warrior priests") were once again harassed by government forces, finding further reason to perfect their fighting skills and make use of their knowledge of ninjutsu.

Though the establishment of a strong central government based on the magnificent Chinese system—and following the precepts of Buddhism—would seem to suggest that tranquility and piety prevailed, that was not at all the case. The Japanese were still close to a primitive tribal society. The Emperor Yozei, for example, was reported to have made peasants climb trees so he could shoot them down with his bow and arrow. He would beat people unmercifully with whips, and it was said he would grab young girls in the streets, tie them with rope and throw them into ponds, watching with glee as they drowned. It's no wonder that small, vulnerable groups like the *yamabushi* felt it necessary to develop their talents as fighters.

The Heian Period (794–1192) was considered by most historians to be the Golden Age of Japan. The center of government was moved from Nara to Kyoto. The new civilization flourished and with it, a new class of wealthy, privileged families like the Taira, Fujiwara, Minamoto and Sugawara. These families, according to Will Durant in *The Story of Civilization:* "Part I, Our Oriental Heritage," ". . . made and unmade emperors and fought with one another in the lusty manner of the Italian Renaissance."

The need for spies, informants and now assassins grew as these families dueled for power. They were new to their wealth and fearful of being toppled from their lofty positions. They were suspicious, envious and devious and would resort to any measures to eliminate threats. Therefore, practitioners of ninjutsu were in great demand, and the art became firmly established and bloomed during this time. Iga Province, close to Kyoto, came under the rule of the Hattori Clan at about the middle of this period; they learned the art from the mountain priests, laying the foundations for the Iga School of Ninjutsu. The ninja was born.

The luxurious living that began in the Golden Age, the great passion for fine clothes, elegant foods, magnificent homes and jewelry, was responsible for the gradual decline of power of the emperor and his court. Lords and ladies became so involved in satisfying their own desires, they completely forgot or ignored their responsibilities to the State. Important government positions were filled by incompetent poets. Corruption spread as offices were sold to the highest bidder. As the rich grew richer, the poor, desperate and helpless, turned to crime. Gangs of bandits roamed freely through the provinces, and in Kyoto, a robber who was said to be a student of ninjutsu lived like a lord, much too powerful to fear attack or arrest. The court had ignored the martial arts in favor of literature and luxury. It no longer had the means to enforce its will. As the power of the emperor declined, the strength of the local lords grew.

By 1160, local groups, usually led by someone who was of imperial descent who had moved to the provinces in search of his fortune, began to exercise authority. They began to build armies and establish alliances for mutual protection. The study of the martial arts was now of paramount importance. Budo schools were established to train a warrior class (the samurai), and ninjutsu was studied to produce the secret agents so necessary to their feudal society. The warriors learned to fight from horseback, using sword and bow and arrow, wearing armor . . . much like the European knights. But there were also those who studied apart to learn the secrets of infiltration and surprise attack.

By the time Yoritomo, a member of the Minamoto Clan (one of the imperial families) revolted, took power and declared himself the first shogun ("general of the emperor's army") in 1192, the ninja turned out by the few schools that existed in Iga Province were regularly used as spies and saboteurs.

Yoritomo died in 1198, after being thrown by his horse when he supposedly saw the ghost of the brother he had murdered. The tales tell that he was actually killed by a ninja hired by one of his enemies.

The Kamakura Period (1192–1333) proved to be the Golden Age of Ninjutsu. The constant conflicts between lords jockeying for power for religious or political reasons provided the perfect setting for the talents of the ninja. Many schools sprang up in Iga and Koga provinces, the centers of ninjutsu learning. One historian suggests there were over fifty ninjutsu families in Koga Province forming the Koga School of Ninjutsu, while the Hattori and Oe clans ruled Iga Province.

As the use of ninja increased, so did the stories of their superhuman abilities. This reputation, according to Steve Hayes, was often propagated by the ninja themselves. Because they were a comparatively weak people, vulnerable to attack by the many warring families around them, it was to their advantage to have others think of them as being gifted with amazing powers. They wanted potential attackers to believe they had the strength of ten men, could turn themselves into all sorts of fierce animals, fly like birds and become invisible at will.

The Kamakura Period also saw the rise of the samurai. It can be said that the ninja were counterculture to the samurai. The stronger the warrior class grew, the greater need there was for the ninja who, like vampires, were nourished by the blood of the samurai.

For the next four centuries, Japan was an armed camp composed of many powerful armies. Though there were periods of relative peace and great prosperity, warfare seemed to be the major occupation. When you consider that Japan had a population of twenty-five million in the sixteenth century (as compared to sixteen million in France, seven million in Spain and about four million in England), with over one million samurai in service supported by over a million vassals or "foot soldiers" (a good ten percent of the population), you can imagine how much attention was given to battle and strategy. Try to imagine the United States with twenty-three million men under arms today and you can get a good idea of just how militaristic a nation Japan was then. According to Durant, "The basic principle of Japanese feudal society was that every gentleman was a soldier, and every soldier a gentleman."

With the introduction of Zen, a form of Buddhism that placed emphasis on rigid physical and spiritual disciplines to achieve enlightenment, in the thirteenth century, the samurai found the basis for their culture—their Code of Conduct (Bushido, the Way of the Warrior). And to fully appreciate the abilities of the ninja, we must know something of this culture and how dedicated and formidable a warrior the samurai was.

The samurai's whole existence was devoted to the military virtues of courage, honor, self-discipline, all bolstered by a complete lack of concern for death. His sword was his soul, and he used it often and with great expertise. If a peasant failed to bow or offended him, he would cut off his head; if he wanted to test the blade of a new sword, he would cut down a man or dog on the street.

The samurai were expected to "die when it was right to die, to strike when it was right to strike." They gambled and brawled and fought for the love of fighting. They were completely loyal to their masters and considered it a privilege to fight and

die for them. If they failed or were unfaithful to
their code of honor, they would stoically commit
seppuku, the more "polite" term for hara-kiri.
Often, on the death of their lord, they would perform ritual suicide so they could serve and protect
their master in the other world. Just before the
Shogun Iyemitsu died in 1651, he reminded his
prime minister, Hotto, of his duties as a samurai.
The minister killed himself immediately.

Perhaps the most famous example of the samurai's loyalty and devotion is the story of the forty-
seven *ronin* ("samurai without masters"). The
incident occurred sometime around 1700. During
an argument between two lords on the castle
grounds at Edo (now Tokyo), one drew his sword
and wounded the other, a man named Kotsuké no
Suké. The drawing of a sword on imperial grounds
was an offense punishable by death. The lord was
ordered to commit *seppuku.* Forty-seven of his
samurai, now *ronin,* waited patiently for two
years, until Kotsuké no longer expected an act of
revenge. They then attacked, killed and cut off
the head of the man who had offended their
master, placed the head on their lord's grave, and
then, because they had flouted the authority of
the court, they all committed hara-kiri.

These are the men the ninja had to meet and
overcome to complete their missions successfully.

As the samurai war-machine developed, so did
the organization of the ninja.

The ninja hierarchy was composed of three
levels. On the lower level were the *genin,* the actual operative agents who possessed the skills necessary to get the job done. They were the spies
and saboteurs, well trained in weapons, martial
arts and disguises. Their immediate supervisors

were the *chunin,* or the organizers. Based on their past experience as *genin,* these men were administrators and planners. The *jonin* were on the highest level; they were the leaders of the families who followed and preached the philosophies of the mountain mystics who first developed ninjutsu—the philosophy that taught ninjutsu as a method of total enlightenment.

These leaders, the *jonin,* understood that total enlightenment tends to point out the discrepancies and imbalances that exist in the world, and that those who are enlightened are misunderstood and feared by those who are not. So the leaders recognized the need for martial emphasis as protection against those who feared them, but they didn't originally develop their warrior talents for aggressive purposes.

The degeneration of the system came about when the *chunin* and *genin* broke from the *jonin* and chose to devote all their energies to military and espionage activities rather than to the original philosophical tenets. The samurai threatened their culture and existence, they reasoned, so they developed only those talents that could meet and neutralize that threat.

By 1333, the power of the Hojo Regency of the Kamakura Period began to disintegrate for the same reason the emperors had forfeited their rights to rule. The heirs of the powerful first shoguns proved to be incompetent cowards and fools. Takatoki, the last of the Hojo line, collected dogs instead of taxes and had four thousand of them, pampered and treated better than his subjects, at the time he was overthrown by the Emperor Go Daigo with the help of the Minamoto and Ashikaga clans. Takatoki and 870 of his retainers took the only honorable exit open to them. They all committed hara-kiri.

Ashikaga then betrayed the emperor, as was often the case with warlords, using magnificent battlefield strategy and the treachery supplied by bands of ninja he employed. The secret agents infiltrated Go Daigo's camp, disrupted his forces with rumor and sabotage, and even killed one of their own number when they suspected that he was on the verge of betraying their warlord. The ninja became Ashikaga's eyes and ears, and they performed all those devious jobs that were beyond the ken of his field warriors.

As the years passed, the Ashikaga shogunate became fat and lazy, turning away from the martial arts and strong, effective government in favor of pleasure. Chaos and civil war once again returned. It was at this time that three great warlords (called powerful robbers by some historians) made their appearance to attempt to bring stability to Japan.

Nobunaga Oda, supported by his two generals, Ieyasu Tokugawa and Hideyoshi Toyotomi, was the first to try. With the help of guns, firelocks introduced by the Portuguese, he was able to swallow up many of the smaller domains and destroy a majority of the weaker warlords. By 1568, he seized control of the imperial and shogunal courts in Kyoto and began his drive against the Buddhists, whom he hated. The ninja, devout Buddhists because of their early association with the mountain priests who developed ninjutsu, found themselves in a battle for survival. The ninja failed in their attempts to assassinate Nobunaga, and he, in retaliation in 1581, invaded the province of Iga and almost totally annihilated the greatly outnumbered (twelve-to-one) ninja force. Many were killed in battle, and those that were captured were brutally tortured in the popular ways of the time: by crucifixion, boiling in oil or water, or being sawed in half from the neck to the groin. The few that escaped scattered through Japan and later served warlords in other areas.

Nobunaga broke the military might of the Tendai stronghold on Mount Hiei and other powerful monasteries with comparative ease, but he never did win major control over Japan because he was assassinated by one of his lords in 1582.

General Ieyasu Tokugawa was near Osaka at the time of Nobunaga's death (the warlord's forces had captured the temple-castle of the True Pure Land sect in Osaka after a ten-year siege). He feared he would be attacked by the warriors of Akechi, the man who had killed Nobunaga, and was able to obtain the help of the famed ninja, Hanzo Hattori, and his clan as bodyguards for his return home.

Ieyasu rewarded Hanzo by placing him and his men on his staff, using them to care for his gardens during peaceful periods and as spies and agents when there was cause for suspicion or threat of conflict. Hanzo was disappointed, though, because he had hoped to be elevated to the noble rank of samurai; this honor was never bestowed upon him by Ieyasu.

Hideyoshi assumed control after Nobunaga's death and in three years made himself ruler of more than half the empire. With a vast army under his control and very little for them to do, the warlord embarked on a campaign to conquer China and Korea. Many thousands of Japanese warriors died, mostly at sea, because of Korean "turtle ships," the world's first ironclads. These invulnerable warships sank or beached over 120 Japanese vessels in one day, killing more than 70,000 warriors. The death of Hideyoshi in 1598 brought an end to this attempt at world conquest, and Ieyasu assumed the leadership of Japan.

Ieyasu made full and constant use of the ninja. In peace they served as his bodyguards or gardeners; during the campaigns, they were once again spies and saboteurs. Ieyasu had sworn a blood oath with Hideyoshi that he would recognize his son, Hideyori, as heir to the Regency of Japan. But Ieyasu declared the oath invalid because he had taken the blood from behind his ear rather than from his fingers or gums as required by the code of the samurai.

Ieyasu was a ruthless leader. He attacked and defeated Hideyoshi's son, forcing him to commit hara-kiri. He then killed all of Hideyori's children, whether legitimate or illegitimate, so there would be no future threat to his rule. He sent his ninja to spy on and assassinate all those he suspected of treason. He tested his retainers or provincial leaders by having ninja feed them false rumors or information to see how they would react. He was a completely amoral man, at one time forcing a subject to commit hara-kiri when he learned the man had killed another for his wife, and then taking the woman himself and making her one of his concubines.

But he was a brilliant leader, and he built the feudal system in Japan until it was the strongest of its type ever known. And the ninja played an important role in his program.

In 1614, he issued an edict forbidding the practice of Christianity and ordered all Christians either to leave the country or renounce their faith. But he did nothing openly to harm them.

In 1638, after his death, his grandson, Iyemitsu, sent a large force with a handful of ninja as spies and saboteurs, to destroy the last remaining fortified enclave controlled by the Christians on the peninsula of Shimabara. There were 38,000 Christians in the stronghold, but after a three-month siege and a brutal attack, all but 105 were massacred. It is said that the ninja infiltrators were responsible for much of the confusion and sabotage that weakened the fortress.

This was the last military campaign in which ninja were used. As peace settled over Japan, the need for samurai and ninja diminished. The samurai were slowly and carefully weaned from military activities and introduced to the arts. In later years they would become some of the finest writers, poets and artists in Japan.

Without the samurai, there was little need for the ninja, and more and more these desperate men turned to any endeavor that would support them. Some became farmers, a large group was put to work as policemen, and others turned to crime. Those who turned to police work found that their espionage training made them excellent criminal investigators; those who chose the other side of the law found their knowledge made them successful, hard-to-catch criminals.

There is one further recorded official use of the ninja by the Japanese government. When Commodore Perry went to Japan in 1854 with a large naval squadron, ninja, operating very much like today's frogmen, boarded the commodore's ship to learn what his intentions were. They were successful in getting on board and leaving unseen, but their mission proved to be unsuccessful because of ·their inability to read or understand English. They searched through the commodore's papers and listened to members of the crew talking, but they didn't understand a word.

Strict laws control the training of ninja today in Japan, and there are <u>few schools in existence</u>. <u>The largest, the Togakure Ryu, run by Dr. Masaaki Hatsumi in Japan and Steve Hayes in the United States</u>, tends to shun the more brutal aspects of ninjutsu and emphasizes in its teachings the spiritual side of the art. But there is no doubt that there are ninja today who practice the physical—the more brutal and devious—teachings of ninjutsu. Just how many active ninja there are is anyone's guess. Secrecy, for the most part, is still at the heart of their art.

Chapter 3

A MIND AND BODY OF IRON

The boy, armed only with a *hyunku,* a small bow, was perched on a cherry tree deep in the heavily wooded mountain region of Iga. He had arrived there alone late that afternoon, just at nightfall, and had climbed up to his position.

Now the night was black, the moon hidden behind clouds. The sounds of the forest surrounded him. Among those sounds he detected potential danger: the guttural growl of a wild dog, fairly close. And earlier he had heard something slithering through the tree below him.

It was the kind of situation that would have raised gooseflesh, or at least given a grown man pause. But the boy was not afraid. Quite the contrary, he welcomed the opportunity to test himself and the skills that he had learned. Now he was free. Now he was ninja.

He listened. Not just listened. *Listened.* It was an acquired skill. He listened not only to the sound coming from without, but also those coming from within: his breathing, his incredibly slow heartbeat.

His *hanshi,* or master, at the *ryu* had told him that darkness was the time of the ninja, and many times he would be waiting in it; the success of his mission or his survival could depend on his ability to remain quiet.

"In the darkness," the *hanshi* had said, "every-one listens better. And they will be listening for you. They must not hear you. You must listen for the sound of yourself and the sound of what is around you."

It was a lesson that did not require emphasis. Once, when he was seven, they brought into the camp the beet-red, partially skinned body of a ninja who had been caught by samurai hiding in a ceiling in a warlord's castle. He had not listened well enough. He had been boiled alive. . . .

This science of listening, based on records of the time, was just one small aspect of the physical (*taiso*) and mental training or conditioning of ninja.

The two processes were intense. They started at the age of five or six and continued until the young man was ready to be a full-fledged ninja, usually in his teens.

While intensity was the order of the day, the regimen would vary according to the particular *ryu.* It would almost certainly include running and walking to build wind and stamina. Often, ninja would have to travel great distances quickly, such as when transporting espionage materials. Incredible as it may seem, historians confirm that some ninja would travel as much as one hundred miles per day. To put this in perspective, elite American troops, such as those in the airborne, might travel twenty-five miles per day. And crack marathoners run twenty-five to twenty-six miles in a little over two hours. It would take them around nine hours (assuming they could run all the way) to travel that same one hundred miles.

Ninja were also trained in specialized ways to walk. For example, they were trained in the method of *yoko-aruki,* or sideways walking. So, they might be tracked across country, but it is said they were able to produce a series of footprints that would confuse their pursuers.

Yoko-aruki was also useful when they were pursued down narrow castle corridors by samurai. The average ninja could travel as fast sideways as a man could trot.

Another unusual way of ninja walking was called *nuki-ashi,* or stealthy step. This was an extremely important skill because so much of the ninja's success depended on it.

Warlords constantly sought to trap the ninja. One way was to leave a board loose near an entryway or in a corridor. When the ninja stepped on it, the board would squeak and alert the guards.

Another primitive alarm was to extend a string with a bell on it across a corridor at ankle height. A ninja stepping into this would make the bell tinkle—and invite disaster.

But ninja were trained to step carefully and *lightly.* To train for this, wet paper about the density of toilet paper was spread on the floor, and ninja trainees were required to walk on it without the soles of their feet picking it up.

Strength was important to a ninja for a variety of reasons. It was related to their skill at martial arts and with the sword, *bo* ("staff"), and a variety of other weapons. A ninja often had to scale sheer walls and other structures where arm strength was particularly important. They had a number of difficult exercises which developed such strength considerably.

One was a kind of push-up. The ninja trainee would lie flat on his stomach, then do a push-up using only his toes and his fingers as support, the arms fully extended. This would create tremendous stress on the arms as well as on the abdomen. Ninja could commonly do it but today it is still considered extremely difficult by physical education instructors.

A not-so-ordinary pull-up was another favored exercise. The bar was gripped with the backs of the hands facing the man. This builds formidable forearm strength. It enabled the ninja to travel hand-over-hand for great distances up, say, the side of a castle wall or to hike his body up a rope secured to a wall.

Ninja had a habit of going that one step beyond the point at which you would think they would stop, and this posture also showed up in exercise. Amazingly enough, they could do repetitive one-arm pull-ups. Even for well-conditioned men, two-arm pull-ups are difficult, but one-arm pull-ups are something else. To get an idea of the difficulty, picture yourself hanging by one arm from a bar or tree limb and then lifting your body straight up until your chin goes over the bar or limb. Ninja did it tens of times in a row—with either arm.

Ninja also believed that the body must be limber, the muscles supple and bendable, and joints dislocatable.

Aside from the general health and conditioning

benefits, a limber body was particularly useful to ninja in achieving "invisibility." It enabled him to form his body into various shapes such as rolling himself up into a ball to simulate a boulder to blend into the landscape or dropping his head on his chest and holding his arms rigid against his sides to simulate a fence shape.

In his manual, "Ninja Combat Method," American ninja Steve Hayes shows a variety of loosening-up exercises including neck rotation, body twist (its action is not unlike the dance of the same name), leg stretch, arm twist, and balance postures. There is nothing unusual about these actions, but if one repeats them they work well.

The ninja ability to dislocate their shoulders at will could be extremely useful if they were bound. If left alone, they could dislocate either shoulder and create slack in the binding, thereby freeing their hands enough to untie themselves. This method of dislocation was the same method used by escape artist Harry Houdini to get out of strait-jackets.

Dislocation was also useful if a ninja wanted to play dead. He could dislocate a shoulder and throw his head off at an odd angle. This action, coupled with a barely perceptible breathing pattern, would often save his life. According to Andrew Adams, in his book *Ninja: The Invisible Assassins,* ninja could also dislocate their jaws, useful in keeping themselves from talking under the stress of torture.

Balance was another important skill to the ninja, whose missions often had him walking along narrow ledges or the tops of walls or roofs and other places more suited to mountain goats. To develop a good sense of balance a favorite ninja training device was to <u>strap on wooden clogs and walk on ice</u>. It is more difficult than ice-skating for the first time, but paid more than its share of dividends on a dark night atop the slimy wall of an enemy castle forty feet above, say, a spike-filled moat.

Ninja were expert at escaping. Indeed, as will be seen in detail in Chapter Nine, they were often so expert that they weren't even seen. However, they were trained in a number of other specific stratagems, all ready to go, as it were, if the enemy got very close.

One, of course—the main one—was the use of *tetsu-bishi,* <u>miniature spiked "mines" which the ninja would sprinkle on the floor behind him</u>. This would play havoc with the feet of the pursuers.

Another favorite of a ninja who was being pursued down a seamless floor of some type was to throw water on it. Such a floor would then assume the traction capabilities of ice.

Coins were also used. A small handful thrown into the face of an attacker would stun him and give the ninja the moment he needed.

In a variation on this gambit, ninja might flip money down on a crowded street. The natural inclination of the people nearby would be to scurry for the money—and form a nice wedge to stop those in pursuit.

<u>Ball bearings</u> were not known in the feudal ninja's day, but they are now used against pursuers. Picture yourself trying to run down a hall, the floor of which is covered with <u>marbles,</u> and you can get an idea of their effectiveness.

Another aid to escape was soil or sand. A handful of this tossed in someone's face could be very effective indeed. <u>The average ninja also carried a</u>

kind of blinding powder. This would stop a pursuer dead in his tracks. Indeed, the knowledge that a ninja might be carrying a blinding powder might give pause because some of the powders caused permanent damage to the eyes.

If possible, the ninja would also keep the sun at his back when fighting or attempting to escape. If the sun was low in the sky and at the right angle it could create a momentary problem with the pursuer's ability to see.

Some writers have also said that ninja were fond of tossing insects and small animals at their pursuers, but there are no details on how the ninja worked out the mechanics of this operation.

Scaling walls and the like was another aspect of ninja training which was very important. He was taught how to set up and climb a variety of ladders, both portable and rigid, as well as the best way to climb a rope. Today, this tradition is still continued at the Togakure Ryu. The combat manual counsels fledgling ninja as follows when climbing a rope: "Position the hanging rope along the inside of your right thigh, running behind your knee and along the outside of your calf, and back across your instep. Press your left foot arch into the rope across your right instep to grip the rope and support yourself. At the same time grip the rope with your hands. Relax the grip of your feet, without disengaging them from the rope. Bend the knees, sliding the feet up the rope, and regrip with the feet. Straighten the knees and work the hands to a higher grip on the rope."

The manual also shows how to make a climbing ladder from a rope—tying loops in it to form hand as well as foot holds. In either case, using a rope with or without the loop, the manual advises that

"The ninja keep the body close to the rope, with the back straight and arms close to the body. This will prevent swinging, which occurs when the arms are straightened and the body is allowed to lean back."

The ninja diet was not extraordinary . . . but it was nothing like the American diet. It was rich in high-protein foods which provide quick energy. Bleached rice, wheat flour, and fish—both trout and bonito—and soybean were staples. Food would be dried or otherwise preserved, then rolled into balls or cut up so that it could be carried long distances.

Ninja sometimes carried a kind of condensed food. As Donn Draeger points out in *Ninjutsu, the Art of Invisibility,* compounded tablets were the ninja's food rations, being both light in weight and space-saving. The actual ingredients for these tablets were considered secret, but most of them contained buckwheat flour, wheat germ, potato flour, Job's tears, carrots and a kind of grass.

The ninja might not be near potable water for long stretches of time, or he might not have the time to stop, or he might fear the water was poisoned, so he also carried with him thirst quenchers. Andrew Adams points out that these included peppermint powder and *umeboshi,* or salted plums. It was also said that sesame seeds were good for slaking thirst. Another trick was to coat the inside of the nostrils with the juice of a leek.

Ninja were also very much concerned with good eyesight and consumed great quantities of Vitamin A via watercress, which grew in abundance by streams.

A ninja's mental conditioning was part and parcel of his physical conditioning. The things that he had to do as he grew up—from learning to dislocate his shoulders to spending nights listening in the wild—made of his mind what he made of his body: iron. It taught him, in clear terms, what he was capable of—and not capable of.

Beyond this, though, special emphasis was put on concentration, what karateka call *ki*, an inner spiritual resource that will drive a person to do things that he might not ordinarily be able to do.

There are the stories told of Bruce Lee, a man only 5′ 8″ and weighing less than 150 pounds, who was able to muster a tremendous amount of power from *ki*. For example, he once held his fist an *inch* from the chest of a 225-pound football player and then struck, knocking the man off his feet.

Karateka commonly break bricks, blocks of wood, stone and blocks of ice with their bare hands; they credit *ki*. Perhaps most instructive of the power of this mental resource was the story told by a Zen master who was out walking with his pupils. A fox was observed in hot pursuit of a rabbit. The Zen master immediately commented that the hare would outrun the fox and the pupils were puzzled. "The fox is faster than the hare," said one of them. "It doesn't matter," said the master, "the rabbit will win." When asked how this could be, the master answered simply, "Because the fox is running for its dinner, but the hare is running for its life."

This *ki*, this "internal" or life "force," is something that ninja hanshi cultivated and developed in the young men under their tutelage. Ninja, hanshi knew, would almost always be outnumbered, and such a mental resource could well prove invaluable.

Another part of a ninja's training which defies, really, total explanation was the development of a sixth sense, a kind of ESP which could tell the ninja a variety of things, such as when a samurai was waiting just around the corner, *katana* upraised, ready to cleave the ninja; when he wasn't alone in a room; tell him, really, that something was not right, and that he had better be alert and aware.

This tradition of teaching is continued today at the Togakure Ryu of Stephen Hayes. The training in the development of this sense is quite specific and detailed. It is not simple to define precisely what this sense is, but in his new book, *Ninja: Spirit of the Shadow Warrior,* Hayes calls it a cosmic consciousness, a reality beyond the mind and its processes; "a third realm of reality . . . is filtered through the mind and defined in ways that are understandable and acceptable to the physical organism."

Hayes says that with proper training people can tie into the "natural laws" which govern everything and thereby sense physical reality when only thought can be detected by the ordinary senses.

In the exercises designed to increase this awareness, there is both a controller —a person who sends signals—and a receiver. One exercise, for example, develops an "open state of mind" by having the receiver jump and otherwise physically react to commands from the controller. To learn how to sense the presence of others, the student stands in a room in which there are few physical distractions and ultimately reduces his physical functions (by controlled breathing and the like) until his "body is surrounded by its own radar-like force field." The controller slowly raises his arm until it is about a hand's length from the face of the receiver. The receiver, who has his eyes closed, tells the controller when he senses the hand.

The exercises proceed until a person is finely tuned. For example, from a number of controllers, the receiver is supposed to sense which one is his by a subtle facial signal. Once the controller is selected, the regular exercise begins.

To train the ninja in "picking up the thoughts of others," a pack of special cards imprinted with symbols is used which the receiver and controller match in an ESP-like exercise.

The major factor, as Steve Hayes points out, separating the ninja combat techniques, and therefore the training, from others is the concept of *kyojutsu ten kan ho,* or <u>deception strategy</u>. Literally translated as "the method of presenting falsehood as truth," this strategy is applied to all of the ninja's activity. It is a balancing of the elements of *in* and *yo* (the yin and yang of China or the plus and minus of the Western world) and makes use of the psychology of preparing an adversary to think in one manner, and then approaching him in another.

Ninja unarmed fighting illustrates this. "Examine yourself in the mirror," says Hayes in his "Ninja Combat Method," "to see how your body looks as you prepare for and deliver a high punch. At the moment it becomes obvious that you are punching high, drop your shoulder and punch to your adversary's ribs or stomach. In a close clash, where fists have turned into grappling hands, pull your adversary toward you. He will probably instinctively try to pull away. As you feel his pull, change your motion to a push while stepping behind his foot and throwing him to the ground. As you begin an attack, wind up and start a punch at your adversary's face. As he brings his forearm up to block, change your fist to a knife-hand and slash into the target his forearm presents."

Hayes also offers some examples of this *kyojutsu ten kan ho* when it comes to blade fighting. "As you slash at your adversary's head with a sword or long knife, and he attempts to block with a blade or metal bar, pull in suddenly and let the tip of your blade catch his forearm or hand. A blade could also be concealed behind the arm by gripping the handle in an underhanded manner with the blade extending up behind the back of the elbow."

As detailed in Chapter Nine, Invisibility, *kyojutsu ten kan ho* was often used in escape and other diversionary tactics. For example, throwing a heavy stone into a moat or river, the ninja could cause a pursuer to assume he was in the water because of the sound or the ripples, and the ninja wouldn't be. Another trick: A ninja might rush up to a group of castle guards with a calamitous tale which, hopefully, would drive the guards off their posts for a moment so the ninja could slip in.

Another aspect of this deception strategy was the appearance of being off guard, unsuspicious. This would be a good way, Hayes says, to use a certified traitor within an organization. The ninja would not indicate any suspicion at all; he could then feed the traitor false information which he, in turn, would feed to his contact.

Another trap which evinces the ninja approach

to combat would be to ensure that a camp looks slovenly and unprepared for action. This could lure the enemy into battle.

Despite the American image of the Japanese today as a people who have invaded America with Hondas rather than cannon, a central fact remains about their culture: It is militaristic and the pages of their history are bloody indeed.

At no time was this more true than during the four hundred years in which the ninja flourished. Death reigned supreme, and if a person could not deal with it, he could not survive.

Early in their lives, ninja children were taught to accept the concept of death. Besides the normal mortality—which of course was much higher in those days than today—there were times when ninja did not return to camp. There were instances where ninja committed public hara-kiri at which children were present.

Training to accept death was no fetish. It related, on the deepest level, to a man's fear and, therefore, his ability as a warrior.

One of the great samurai fighters of the day, Miyamoto Musashi, expressed this philosophy in his classic fighting "bible," *Book of the Five Rings, a Guide to Strategy.* He says that the warrior should keep himself ". . . accustomed to the idea of death and resolved on death, and consider yourself as a dead body; thus becoming one with the way of the warrior, you can pass through life with no possibility of failure and perform your office properly."

It is evident that the ninja did consider himself a walking dead man.

Ninja regularly would not only lose their lives in battle, but would kill themselves to avoid capture and torture. Indeed, one gets the feeling that a ninja, far from being afraid of death, somehow regarded it as a friend—a friend that, he knew, he would inevitably meet sooner than most men. And, true to say, a friend that he would also introduce many others to prematurely.

Besides all of the above, ninja were well trained in other skills of ninjutsu—including martial arts, poisons, espionage, stratagems, invisibility and a stunning array of weapons. In the end, a fully trained ninja at, say, the age of seventeen, was one of the most formidable fighting machines ever created.

Chapter 4

KUJI-IN: ENERGY AND POWER
THROUGH THE HANDS

At the very heart of ninja training and life is the
development of spiritual and mental strength. To
the ninja, knowledge of the physical aspects of
his art—his capabilities with weapons and as an
empty-hand fighter—was not enough to make
him the complete warrior and certainly not enough
to make him the complete man. He also had to
have acute insight, the ability to perceive and
understand all that emanated from within himself
and from the environment around him. He had to
be completely aware of the energies he possessed
and know how to harness and use them effectively. Toward this end, he adopted the *kuji-in*, finger-
entwining hand positions that were supposedly
able to channel energy. These hand positions were
taken from the *mudras* ("hand signs") of Indian
and Tibetan esoteric lore and were a part of advanced meditative practices used by these early
Buddhists.

When the Emperor Kwammu of Japan sought

a greater knowledge of Buddhism (some historians claim he was attempting to reform the Buddhist Church), he ordered a monk, Dengyo Daishi, who lived on Mount Hiei near Kyoto, to visit China and study the secret doctrines being taught on Mount T'ien-T'ai. A young monk who accompanied him paid particular attention to the doctrines of the mystical sect called Mikkyo, also known as Shingon, the "secret knowledge" or "true word."

The young monk, who was known after his death as Kobo Daishi, returned to spread this new knowledge which, because it was so profound and used a great deal of pomp and ceremony in its worship, became fairly popular in certain areas of Japan. Those who chose to follow this new sect, many of whom would later become ninja, were considered mystics because they believed they knew the secret that would allow them to achieve the nature of Buddha during their lifetime, the spiritual and moral methods of attaining enlightenment.

In his "Shadows of Iga" newsletter, Steve Hayes suggests that Mikkyo also came to Japan through the teachings of wandering monks, warriors and scholars who fled their native China after the fall of the T'ang Dynasty.

"In feudal Japan," he says, "the teachings were transmitted as a body of knowledge that stressed the power inherent in the individual person. Not a religion, but a working set of principles or universal laws, the teachings of Mikkyo were taken to heart and practiced rigorously by a segment of Japanese society that later became the forerunners of the ninja." It is the opinion of Hayes that the form of Mikkyo that stressed ornate trappings and complex rituals was not the Mikkyo of the ninja. "As ninja," he says, "we are not interested in or associated with any religion." Certainly this is a different interpretation of Mikkyo, but one that might explain why the ninja were so persecuted during the religious wars and why they had to develop their fighting talents and become the Shadow Warriors of Japan.

The *kuji-in* helped the ninja build confidence and strength. Some claim they would also help the ninja sense hidden danger or foresee death. The ninja's Mikkyo taught that certain electro-polar channels or meridians of the body are most sensitive in the hands and feet. The *kuji-in*, or hand positions, provide a control system based on a balancing or directing of energy through the hands. In this system, the thumb represents the source of power *(Ku)*, and each of the fingers represents one of the four elemental manifestations: *Chi* (earth—solids), *Sui* (water-liquids), *Ka* (fire—combustion) and *Fu* (wind—gases). Different energies of the body are represented by these five "element" codes. It was the belief of the ninja that hand positions, with concentration and stress on the various energies (fingers), could bring about an alteration in the body's moods and capabilities at any given moment.

Two of the hand positions are shown here, but it must be stressed that these are just illustrations and can't be considered a lesson in *kuji-in*. Simply folding the fingers briefly will not produce any effect on the personality or help you produce power. To develop a control over the subtle energies of the body requires a considerable amount of study and concentration. There are also related mental and breathing processes which have not been included here and can be directed only by an experienced teacher. What we show here is just one more facet of the ninja psychology and training so we can better understand the great power of this amazing warrior.

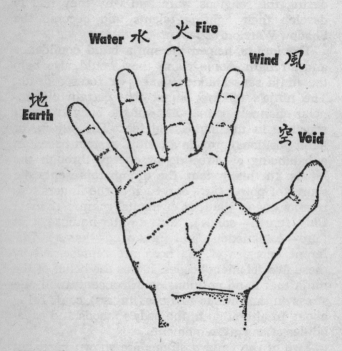

(Figure 1)
The right hand is known as the positive or power hand. The left hand is the negative or receptive hand. The thumb represents the *Ku* (void) element and is the source of power (creativity). The first finger represents the element *Fu* (wind —gases) and controls wisdom (benevolence); the second is *Ka* (fire—combustion) and represents intellect (aggression); the third is *Sui* (water—liquids) and works on the emotions (adaptability); the fourth is *Chi* (Earth—solids) and covers the physical body (stability).

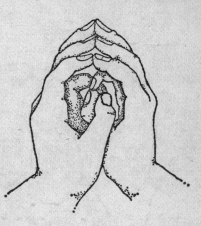

(Figure 2)

CHI NO RIN—"Earth Ring of Power"

To encourage more of an earth-inspired stability and strength, the little finger is curled to form a ring with the folded thumb. This little-finger-and-thumb ring is interlocked with the little-finger-and-thumb ring of the other hand, and the pointer, middle and ring fingertips are pressed together. The ninja then concentrates on generating mental and physical strength.

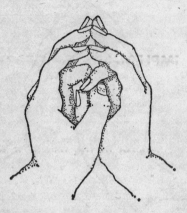

(Figure 3)

SUI NO RIN—"Water Ring of Power"

To encourage more of a water-inspired adaptability, flexibility and power, the ring finger is curled inward to meet the tip of the folded thumb. This ring-finger-and-thumb circle is interlocked with the ring-finger-and-thumb circle of the other hand, and the pointer, middle and little fingertips are pressed together. The ninja then concentrates on generating suppleness and power.

Chapter 5

IMPLEMENTS OF DEATH

Ninja were experts in the use of a wide variety of weapons—more than twenty, by most accounts —including the small and large bow, sword, knives and daggers, primitive cannon and shotgun, *bo* ("staff"), scythe and chain, blowgun and *tonki* (a collection of small, nasty, metal objects like the *shuriken* and calthrop which were used to harass—and sometimes kill—the enemy).

The sword had a much different meaning for the ninja than it did for the samurai. To the latter, the sword was an honorable extension of the man, and it was a formidable, horrific weapon. It was the soul of the samurai.

Samurai carried two swords. The long sword (there were two "big swords" called *daito;* one of them, the *katana,* is the weapon we refer to here) was made of high-carbon steel. It took months to make by smiths who hammered and folded and hammered again until the edge of the blade contained literally millions of layers of finely forged steel. The rest of the blade was of much softer steel so the weapon would be flexible except for the edge, which was hard and amazingly sharp; it was capable of slicing through armor. Such swords lasted hundreds of years and many made during the feudal period still exist.

During World War II, American army training manuals instructed GI's to defend against Japanese wielding *katana* by blocking sword strikes with their rifles. But the manuals had to be revised when it was discovered that the *katana* had no difficulty slicing through these rifles. They are still considered the finest swords ever produced.

The ninja sword, on the other hand, was a bit shorter than the *katana* (twenty-four inches as opposed to twenty-six-and-a-half to thirty-seven inches) and of much poorer quality. It was just another weapon in his arsenal and by comparison to the samurai's sword, its blade edge was dull and its quality nondescript. Because of this difference, the techniques used by the ninja when wielding his sword were in sharp contrast to those used by the samurai. The samurai would swing his sword, cutting off an arm, leg or head with ease. The ninja, on the other hand, would have to swing and then saw into the body once the blade touched flesh in order to achieve reasonable penetration. And because of the relative dullness of his sword, the ninja relied much more on "stabbing" (thrusts) than did the samurai. Both achieved the same goals in the end, but the samurai was able to do it with greater ease. When a ninja had a confrontation with a samurai, he was at a disadvantage if he depended only on his sword. He would generally have available one of the other weapons from his arsenal to "even" the odds.

Even with his weapons, one could see the devilish cleverness of the ninja at work. Weapons had other uses to the ninja than those originally intended. The sword, for example, could be jammed into the earth and its guard used as a step. Also, since the blade was dull enough to grip safely (the ninja could hold it with both hands, his fingers barely touching the cutting edge), the guard could be used as a hook so that he could pull himself upward. Using the samurai sword for the same purpose would produce shaved fingers or bloody stumps.

Even the scabbard of the ninja sword had other uses. It was commonly longer than the length of the blade. In the extra space, the ninja secreted drugs, poisons, darts and other small implements that he used in his work.

The scabbard might also have a removable tip; when this tip was taken off, the scabbard could be used as a snorkel for breathing underwater. It was also used as a probe in a dark room to determine who or what was there. It, rather than the ninja, might be the recipient of a sneaky sword swipe in the darkness.

The staff (*bo* in Japanese) was one of the first weapons developed by man when he realized he would have to fight if he was to survive. The early staff was just a branch from a tree, but it had many advantages over man's oldest weapon, the rock. The rock, once thrown, left a man defenseless; if it were held, it could be used only in close-quarter combat. The tree branch could be thrust and swung to keep an animal or enemy at bay. It was a revolutionary weapon.

The ninja recognized early the versatility of the *bo*, and it became one of the most important weapons in their arsenal. Though the art of the use of the *bo* (*bojutsu*) was popular throughout Japan, it was the ninja, with his cunning and inventiveness, who made the *bo* a weapon of "many parts."

The common *bo* was a staff approximately two inches in diameter and made of hardwood or bamboo, in which case it was hollow. The length of the *bo* varied according to the preference of the user, but it was generally about five feet long.

The solid *bo* could be a fearsome weapon. It was long enough to keep a swordsman at bay and heavy enough to inflict serious injury if it connected. Held so that the space between the hands was a bit wider than the body, the *bo* could be swung either to the right or left, to strike the body or arms, brought down to strike the head or up to connect with the groin or legs. It could be used to sweep a man off his feet or, if thrust like a soldier charging with bayoneted rifle, it could knock the wind out of a man if it caught him in the stomach or kill him if it connected with his sternum or throat.

Though the hollow *bo* was lighter and seemingly less dangerous, it could deliver a telling blow; but it also had a much more deadly side to it.

In open combat, the ninja would assume a stance with the weighted, open end of his *bo* directed toward his opponent. His adversary would, naturally, be concerned with being struck with the weapon. What he would not expect would be a quick flick of the wrist by the ninja. Instantaneously, a poison dart, fired like a bullet from the *bo*, would be sticking out of his forehead.

Or he might get even a bigger surprise . . . a knife in the chest. That same flick of the wrist could make a concealed long knife fly out wickedly at whatever was in its path.

A chain could also be concealed in the hollow *bo*. In this case, one end of the *bo* was capped or covered. As a fight began, the ninja would pull off the cap and release a five- or six-foot chain anchored to the end of the *bo*. He could swing it, disabling or tying up an opponent, and then use the other end of the *bo,* which was suitably weighted, to knock his opponent senseless or kill him. This weapon was called a *shinobi zue*.

The *shinobi zue* could be especially useful when ninja were disguised (and they *were* frequently disguised) as priests. No one would pay any attention to a holy man carrying a staff.

The hollow *bo* could also be loaded with iron balls, which could be fired with great force at a number of enemy.

A close relative to the *bo* is the *jo,* the short stick. About two feet long, this stick has proved to be a very effective offensive and defensive weapon. It is an excellent blocking tool when used against a man with a weapon like a knife or club. Then, depending on where it is held, it can be used to slash, thrust or jab. As a jabbing weapon, the *jo,* held near the striking end and twisted as it connects, can inflict a great deal of damage. The areas of the body that are particularly vulnerable are the solar plexus, throat, nose, chin, back (the spine), the back of the neck and the temples.

Used as a baton, with the wrist as focal point and the stick held firmly in the web of the hand and controlled by the thumb and forefinger (secured by the other three fingers when striking), it becomes a formidable weapon against an opponent charging with a knife.

There are some weapons which the ninja used that can be traced back to their agrarian roots and resemble working tools. One of these is the *kusarigama.* This composite weapon is composed of a sickle (short scythe) attached to a long chain that has a weight at its end. Often, these weights were knobbed or spiked.

This odd-looking weapon is vicious and versatile. In close quarters, the ninja could use the sickle to slash or stab. The blade portion could also be used to hook or block the weapons of attackers. Holding the end of the chain, the sickle could be whirled and thrown at an opponent, or the sickle could be held, and the chain could be whipped out to ensnare an enemy or his weapon. Once he was caught, the ninja would attack with the sickle and finish him off. Quite a simple farm tool!

Similar in its use was the *kyoketsu-shogei*, a knife attached to one end of a long cord made of woman's or horse's hair. At the other end of the cord was a ring. The knife end could be used in close quarters, but if an enemy was at a distance, the ring could be whirled and tossed so that it would wrap around him, tying him up just long enough for the ninja to swing into action and thrust and slash with his knife.

Different people have become associated with different weapons: Indians with bows, cowboys with six-shooters, samurai with their swords . . . and the ninja with *shuriken.*

The *shuriken,* small metal devices, usually in the shape of stars or wheels with sharpened points, were used with chilling effect in the past and are still favorites of "modern" ninja. In films, novels and TV, the *shuriken* is the hallmark of those devious, mysterious men in black. Whenever ninja appear, it is certain the *shuriken* will be the weapon they use most . . . the one we remember.

But in actuality, the *shuriken* were not designed as killing weapons. Though some were large and designed to penetrate deeply, most were relatively small and were used to deter or distract a pursuer while the ninja made his escape. Or they could be used to silently cut the arm or leg of a guard. He would not hear the weapon or see it whiz by. All he would notice would be the pain and the trickle of blood. Enough to draw any man's attention away while the ninja sneaks by and into the castle.

Shuriken were normally used within a range of ten yards. They were tossed either overhand or in a horizontal way, just as one would toss a Frisbee.

Coated with poison, the *shuriken* could be quite deadly, and while they are the most famous, they are just one of a variety of small, metal weapons known collectively as *tonki*, as mentioned earlier.

One of the more inventive and effective of these *tonki*, which probably made its public American debut in the James Bond film, "Casino Royale," are *tetsu-bishi*, or calthrops. These are spiked devices that resemble miniature mines. They were designed so that they would land with one point up and were sprinkled on a road by a ninja as he made his escape. His pursuers, clad in the thin straw sandals that were common footgear in Japan, would step on the calthrops and have to give up the chase, especially if the tips of the points were coated with poison. It was pointed out by one philosopher of the time that once a man had stepped on a *tetsu-bishi* when pursuing a ninja, thereafter "he would step with gentle foot."

Tonki, in the form of poisoned darts, were used in blowguns, and tiny darts and needles were often held by a ninja in his mouth, to be blown in the eyes of an enemy at close range.

Modern ninja have gone the medieval ninja one better in terms of poison pins. Today there are pins and needles as thin as the ones used in acupuncture that are so sharp, they will enter the body and be withdrawn bloodlessly . . . leaving no wound. When such a pin is coated with a hard-to-detect poison, the average coroner would have difficulty coming up with the cause of death.

Ninja women, or *kunoichi,* also used pins with chilling success. They would keep long, poison-tipped pins in their overblown hairdos. When the victim was preoccupied with the sex act, the *kunoichi* would withdraw a pin and, at the right moment, drive it in where it would do the most good.

A number of ninja weapons, as previously mentioned, were multipurpose. They were tools, but also instruments of death. The *shuko,* or "tiger claws," which have been celebrated in fiction and films, also had two purposes. It was a weapon and could be used as an aid to climbing.

Essentially, the *shuko* consisted of a pair of metal pieces joined by a flat band that could be slipped over the hand and tightened. On the palm side of the *shuko* were sharp projections (usually four). In essence, they turned the ninja's hands into sharp claws.

With *shuko,* the hands were now equipped for climbing trees, walls, fences, giving the ninja far more purchase and power than his fingers alone could.

In close combat, the claws became a fierce

weapon . . . one with which a ninja could rip open an enemy's face, chest or groin.

Very similar to the *shuko* were individual animal claws or individual sheaths with claws (called *nekade*) which ninja slipped over their fingers and tied in place. These were also used in climbing and in combat.

Ninja also let their fingernails grow long and thick; a process aided by the consumption of large amounts of gelatinous foods. The nails were then sharpened and could be used as claws. They could be deadly when dipped in poison.

For killing at a distance, the ninja used two types of bows *(yumi):* a small bow for close range and a long bow for both short- and long-range fighting. Like the American Indian, they would use fire arrows and ones rigged with explosives. Firing these into a hard-charging, mounted band was an excellent way to disrupt them.

It was said the ninja could shoot arrows with deadly accuracy, which is not too surprising when one considers that a ninja might have been practicing from the age of four or five. Hakeo Kumasat, a Japanese historian, said, "The average ninja was an Olympic-quality archer."

There was, for instance, the legend of a warlord who lived in the mid–fifteenth century. He was well protected at all times and a number of attempts on his life had proved unsuccessful—mainly because he rarely emerged from the protection of his castle. One day, though, a ninja archer, it is said, succeeded in shooting an arrow some seventy-five yards through a space in a fence, through an open window and into his forehead, killing him instantly. From the ninja's perspective, the target must not have seemed much bigger than a thumbprint.

One of the more unusual weapons, which Andrew Adams describes, was a rudimentary spray gun. It consisted of a length of bamboo about a foot and a half long. One end was closed, except for a small hole. The ninja inserted another piece of bamboo, just big enough to fit inside the first piece, which was filled with poisoned water. When the smaller piece was pushed into the latter, the water would atomize out the small hole and spray the blinding water at an opponent.

Firearms were not all that common a weapon with ninja during most of the tumultuous times in Japan. It was soon after 1542, when the first Europeans, the Portuguese, arrived, that ninja started using them to any degree.

The Portuguese had two arquebuses and ammunition with them (the Japanese called these first guns *Tanegashimans*), and, according to Noel Perrin in his book, *Giving Up the Gun*, "the moment Lord Tokitaka, the feudal master of Tanegashima, saw one of them take aim and shoot a duck, the gun enters Japanese history." The ninja and samurai quickly learned to use guns and it wasn't long before a trained warrior could ring up a perfect score shooting a hundred shots at a target.

But the gun did not last long as a weapon. Within a hundred years it disappeared from the warrior's arsenal for a period of two centuries. The warrior class, the samurai, objected to the weapon because it was truly the "great equalizer" —it made it possible for a lowly farmer to kill a great warlord. It offended the Code of Bushido. And to the ninja, it was a cumbersome weapon, not one that blended well with his life of secrecy and stealth.

However, the ninja did use the gun sometimes and, on occasion, a primitive mortar made from hollowed logs that could be hand held. The problem with this weapon was that it often exploded, doing as much or more damage to the attacker as it did to the victim. There was also a kind of crude shotgun called a *sode tsutsu,* which was said to be effective at close range, though that is debatable.

Ninja also made primitive hand grenades by emptying out the contents of eggs and filling the shells with powder which would explode (flash) when thrown. Modern ninja produce the same effect with a flash paper they have developed.

The *manriki gusari,* a three-foot length of chain weighted at both ends ("ten thousand power chain"), was used often and effectively by ninja, though it was originally developed as a self-defense weapon by a guard at Edo Castle. The *manriki*'s weight and size vary, but they are generally small enough to be easily concealed in the hand or up the sleeve (or in a pocket or sash). The trained user can easily and quickly block the attack of or ensnare an enemy or his weapon. If one end is held in the hand, it can be used as a whip. The weighted end is capable of doing a great deal of damage.

Today, ninja have some very different and exotic weapons.

For example, there are buttons worn on jackets that are actually mini-grenades which can be ripped off and thrown to divert or injure a victim.

Ninja thrive on creating weapons that do not look like weapons. Indeed, not too long ago there was a case reported on television and in the newspapers of a Czechoslovakian journalist who suddenly became ill—and died. His only complaint was that he had been jabbed accidentally on a London street by a man with an umbrella.

After extensive research British scientists uncovered a microscopic hollow ball, inside of which was a gruesomely powerful poison. While this was purportedly the work of the NKVD, its devilish ingenuity had the trademark of the ninja.

There doesn't seem to be any question, though we could not get any official confirmation, that ninja are employed by a number of private and government secret service agencies here and abroad. You can well believe that any ninja employed by these agencies is well trained in the latest weaponry.

Still, there are some quite pedestrian objects liked and used by the ninja. One is an ordinary straw, which made its big debut in the novel *Shibumi*. The author declined to note the way it was used to kill. However, since it is our belief that weapons don't kill but people do, the answer is this: The straw is held with the thumb over one end, then driven toward the object. As it is, a column of air builds up inside the straw, lending it rigidity. We have seen a straw driven like this through a raw potato. This simple drinking straw can be a doubly dangerous weapon when you consider it can also be used as a blowgun.

Chopsticks were also used as weapons by ninja of the past, and are still used by them to this day. A chopstick driven into the side of the neck or other vulnerable area of the face will quickly disable or kill a victim. In the past, the *kogai*, a skewerlike tool carried in the scabbard of the short sword, was separated and used as chopsticks by ninja as well as other warriors, but it was also an effective weapon. It was often used to attack the ankles of an opponent. If the man can't stand, he can't fight. And, as a touch of irony, it was often left in the ear of a dead victim as a sort of gruesome calling card.

One of the favorite weapons of Ron Duncan is the *yawara* stick, a round piece of wood, metal or plastic a bit over an inch in diameter and five or six inches long. The *yawara* can be used in many ways when clutched in the fist of a fighter. First of all, it hardens the hand and makes a punch much more powerful (the way street fighters used a roll of coins to add that extra "zap" to their punches). Then, its protruding ends can be used to apply pressure to the nerves and produce a temporary paralysis. Finally, it can be used to strike at the temple, the upper area of the spine between the shoulder blades, the kidneys and the jaw. Held with one end braced against the palm, it becomes lethal when thrust into the throat, groin or sternum.

"Everything, or most everything, you find around you can be a weapon," says Duncan. "The modern ninja is trained to use many of the things he carries for defense or attack. The keys in his pocket or the ball-point pen in his coat can be used to stab or slash. A tightly rolled newspaper thrust into the throat or chest of a man can put him out of action long enough for you to make your move —to escape or attack. Even a matchbook, properly held and used, can tear the flesh from a man's face."

Somewhat more sophisticated weapons for the modern ninja are being produced by Larry Beaver of Beaver Products. Larry is a student of Steve Hayes, and along with Bud Malmstrom, runs his school in Atlanta, Georgia.

One weapon Larry produces is a short dagger made from a three-cornered file and hidden in a fountain pen. One instance where the sword is definitely mightier than the pen.

A more recent development by Beaver, and one that he is still improving, is a blowgun made from a hollowed pen. Using map pins as darts, this weapon is only effective when used close (twelve to sixteen inches) to the victim. A modern ninja can walk nonchalantly past his victim, seemingly wrapped in thought as he chews on his pen, and send a lethal poisoned dart into his throat without anyone noticing.

It is interesting to note at this point that Larry Beaver is employed by a secret government agency, the name of which he prefers to keep to himself, to teach ninja tactics.

As technology and knowledge grow, so does the arsenal of ninja weapons. Some are sophisticated, some simple . . . some are old, some are new. And there are still many ninja ready to use them.

Chapter 6

TOOLS OF THE TRADE

In addition to carrying a full complement of weapons, ninja were also outfitted with a variety of pieces of equipment that were, for the most part, absolutely necessary to their method of operation. Some of them had that unmistakable touch of ninja inventiveness and, in quite a few cases, could be used as weapons as well as tools.

The uniform (*shinobi shozoko*) of the ninja could be any one of three colors, but most of the time he wore black because it blended with the darkness in which he was most at home. On assignments that required he work in snow, he wore a uniform of white, and if he had to pass unnoticed through a wooded or brush terrain, his clothes would be made from material with a camouflage pattern. This last uniform could be compared to those worn by present-day warriors involved in jungle warfare.

The uniform consisted of a number of garments that allowed a minimum of flesh to show. Indeed, when a ninja was fully clothed, only the eyes and a horizontal slit of the face and hands would be revealed. There were split-toe cotton or straw shoes (split so the big toe was separated from the others, allowing the ninja to climb more easily), trousers, jacket, a hood or scarf that could be used as a mask, and a sash or obi.

The obi had other uses besides holding his sword and other weapons. It could be laid across a noisy floor so the ninja could walk without being heard. And it was also a weapon. It could be used as a garrote and also in empty-hand combat (when the ninja was weaponless, that is) to snare a weapon, tie up an enemy and bring him to the ground, or just swung to divert his attention. There is an entire course of training in the use of the obi as a weapon or for self-defense, and we can be sure the ninja was familiar with most of these techniques.

Not all ninja operations were covert. He sometimes was right out in the open beside the warlord who employed him, and for such occasions he wore chain-mail armor and even a chain-mail undergarment.

The familiar uniform of the ninja had many pockets, both inside and out, to allow him to carry all the tools and weapons he needed on his assignments: from drugs and poisons to chains, ropes, tonki and knives.

Like modern soldiers, a canteen was a standard part of a ninja's equipment. This was usually filled with water or green tea. Another standard piece of equipment was a fire-starter kit. This kit would provide warmth in the winter and could also be useful to fire a flaming arrow shot at a fortress or enemy. Or once he entered a fortress, it could provide the spark needed to "torch" it.

Ninja were realists, so they carried first-aid kits filled with primitive potions and solutions. Sword or knife wounds were expected, and for these he sometimes carried herb root and goose-foot and the cowpea plant. In his book, Andrew Adams notes that these things were "mixed in equal quantities, charred and then painted on the wound." Some wounds, of course, could not be so easily repaired. But the ninja was quite knowledgeable about stopping blood flow with tourniquets and, a method used today that we consider a recent medical development, applying direct pressure to the bleeding wound.

Adams also says the ninja had a cure for cancer—or at least he believed it was a cure. He would grind a piece of the wisteria tree into a powder, mix it with water and drink it.

Besides major maladies or battle wounds, ninja were subject to common ailments such as headaches, sinusitis, sores and toothaches. To alleviate such discomforts, he used an old remedy passed on from China called *Ch'an Su,* the basic ingredient of which was not, as you probably guessed, penicillin, but toad skins.

One of the ninja's main preoccupations was getting into places which were usually well guarded or constructed so as to be difficult to climb or penetrate. For these missions, he had a variety of scaling tools.

Number one was a rope, mainly because it was light and could be easily carried. But this was no ordinary rope. Usually it would have a metal hook at one end which could be varied in construction; some were single-pronged, while others were double- or triple-pronged. The purpose of this tool is obvious. It would be tossed over a wall—hopefully the hook would catch onto the top or a beam or abutment—and the ninja then could pull himself up and over.

Ninja also used ladders. These were far more efficient than the rope and hook when there was a band of men trying to get in and out of a compound quickly. These ladders were also portable, consisting of bamboo or hardwood rungs fastened by metal rings or slips to the rope sides. To get a ladder operational, however, it would first be necessary for one of the ninja to get to the top of the wall by means of a rope and hook. Once there, he would be tossed a rope attached to the top rung of the ladder so that he could pull it up and position and secure it.

The rope for these ladders was made from hemp or some other commonly available fiber. Some, though, were constructed of horse or woman's hair, which proved to be of greater strength. The last thing a ninja needed was to have a ladder or rope break with him twenty feet up the side of a wall.

Another useful scaling tool is one we have discussed as a weapon and one that has made more than an occasional appearance in martial arts films. It is the *shuko*, or tiger claws. These steel climbing bands are strapped to the hands with the claws or spikes on the palm side. They can easily penetrate wood—when the ninja is climbing a tree, the side of a ship or a wooden wall—or they can be hooked over the edges of blocks or in the cracks of stone walls that are scaled. Similar in its use is the *tegaki*, which is a hook strapped to the hand and secured by a metal band tightened around the wrist to hold the hook firmly in place.

As you might expect, these were formidable

climbing aids, especially when you consider that many fortresses during the feudal period had wooden walls. And once a ninja scaled a wall, he didn't worry about a weapon . . . he had one in the palm of each of his hands.

Ninja also used metal foot spikes (*ashiko*) attached to the balls of their feet, making them appear truly like animals. It must have been a stout-hearted guard not to faint dead away when confronted by a black-suited ninja, claws on hands and feet, in the middle of the night.

A variation of the *shuko* were *nekade*. These were individual fur sheaths with real animal claws attached. To use them, the ninja would slip the sheaths over his fingers and strap them in place. They were not only useful in climbing, but when used on an enemy, it made it appear as if he had been clawed to death by a wild animal.

Rigid ladders were also used by ninja, but usually in operations where ninja would be making an all-out assault on a fortress. In covert operations, they would be much too cumbersome to conceal or carry.

Once inside a fortress, a ninja could not generally just proceed to his destination without overcoming some other obstacles. Besides guards, there might well be locked doors. For getting through them he had a variety of tools.

Normally, the most desirable was the lockpick, or *osaku,* because this would let him do the job silently. Failing this, he had a tool very much like a crowbar called a *tsuba-giri;* this did a good job of springing a door and also was very effective at cutting out a lock. If required, the ninja also had in his tool arsenal a form of hacksaw called a *shikoro,* which he could use to slice through metal as well as wood.

Boring holes might also be necessary once inside a fortress, and for this there was the *kunai*. Through these holes the ninja could observe the most intimate activities of a warlord or his retainers and hear information that could be of use to his own lord. Perhaps the most famous story concerning the use of this tool was the one told of the ninja who had bored, from above, through the ceiling of the bedroom of a warlord. He dropped a string through the hole until its end was directly above the mouth of his intended victim. He then poured poison, drop by drop, down the string, but, as the story goes, the warlord closed his mouth just in time to live.

Occasionally, a tool would have a grisly use. There is at least one story on record of a ninja whose foot was caught in an inescapable trap in the floor of a castle. There was no way he could release himself. Finally, out of desperation, he cut off his own foot with his *shikoro* and escaped.

Weapons often did duty as tools. The *kusari-gama,* for example, with its scythelike blade was a natural for digging and cutting, and the knife end of the *kyoketsu-shogei* could also be used for the same purpose. Some *shuriken* had holes in their centers, which made them very useful for removing nails. While the ninja generally needed everything he carried, he would often be overladen with equipment, and he would be quite pleased when he would find a weapon that would also serve him as a tool.

The ninja also had an array of devices to enable him to operate well around water—on top of it and below it. Ninja enjoyed the reputation for being able to walk on water, and a number of these devices certainly would have fostered this impression.

One such device was the *ukidara,* a pair of large airtight pots which the ninja would step into and paddle across the water. While ungainly, and considered ridiculous by some modern-day ninja, these pots *did* work.

Ninja had less success with the *mizugumo* or "water spiders." Each was composed of four pieces of wood fastened together to form a ring. There was also a piece of wood in the center of the ring, secured to the circle by three pieces of rope. The ninja would step on the center boards of these rings and "slide" over the water. The instrument, for obvious reasons, failed more than it worked.

Ninja also had a variety of rafts. There were the *kameikada,* which were made of bamboo or other woods mounted on sealed, watertight jars. There were also *shinobi bune,* which were very small boats that were designed to transport one man.

When pursued, a favorite gambit of the ninja was to submerge himself in water and stay there until his pursuers had given up. Breathing exercises gave him a phenomenal ability to hold his breath, but he also often carried a bamboo pole —a kind of feudal snorkel—which he could use. With or without the snorkel, it was his practice to lie on the bottom in shallow water near the shoreline, his body, and perhaps the tube, hidden by vegetation.

In the winter, it is said by Adams, the ninja even carried his own portable heater—a *doka*— which he kept in one of his pockets. It was made of a shell or hollow iron box into which burning coals were placed. It could be used for both warming the hands and lighting fuses.

Ninja are, of course, thought of as lone operators . . . and for the most part they were. But occasionally, they did operate in small bands or large attack groups, and then they used larger equipment.

For battering down gates, they had a log battering ram as well as a device with which they could swing a large boulder against a door. For spilling troops on top of a wall quickly, they utilized a paddle-wheel–like device. The wheel was parked next to a wall and slowly turned, with ninja jumping off onto the wall when the revolution of the wheel got them close to the top.

Chapter 7

POISON: DEATH IN SMALL DOSES

If any weapon seems in perfect harmony with the being of a ninja, it is poison: it is deceptive in the extreme. One can imagine a ninja watching a man eating or drinking something which has been specially prepared. Suddenly his body starts to swoon or shake or otherwise evince great consternation until, a few minutes later, he is dead. The ninja would take satisfaction in the idea that he had done his job well.

The modern ninja is extremely knowledgeable about poison. He knows the chemistry as well as a pharmacist does. And he knows, like his ancient forebears, *how* to use them: to add to food or drink or to make a knife or perhaps a *tetsu bishi* or dart deadly.

Of course, not all ninja poisons are lethal. Some will merely paralyze.

Yesterday's ninja didn't have all of the sophisticated synthetic poisons of today, but they had organic ones which were extremely deadly.

One is the famous fugu poison which is derived from the blowfish or puffer fish, so called because it puffs up its cheeks when annoyed or searching for food. People are accidentally killed by this poison *every* year in Japan. In one recent year, for example, there were some 250 poisonings attributed to eating blowfish—and half of these unfortunates died.

The problem with accidental poisoning is worst in the winter when the puffer is at its tastiest. The poison is also at its most virulent. Cooks are skilled in not only preparing the puffer for eating, but removing the poison (they are licensed by the government). And it is not easy. The poison, technically known as tetradoxin, stays potent even though the fish is cooked, and only a small amount (eight to ten milligrams) is required to be fatal, and it can be found in any organ of the fish.

It was simple to use a blowfish poison. All the ninja need do was slip a piece of the raw fish onto the plate of the intended victim. The poison attacks the respiratory center in the brain, paralyzing the muscles related to breathing.

Another animal source of poison was the *bufo marinus*, an enormous toad, which also lays claim to being the world's largest, with a body length (not counting legs) of up to nine inches.

The toad's poison is extremely toxic. It causes high blood pressure, headache and paralysis; its effect would be similar to taking uncontrolled amounts of the heart drug digitalis.

The poison, which comes from glands behind the eyes, was used on spear tips, arrows, and darts. To extract the poison, the toad is impaled on a spit and roasted. Blisters form on the skin and as the poison drips out from the glands, it is caught in containers and then fermented.

Scorpions were also said to have been used to dispatch enemies.

A relative of spiders, the scorpion has a wicked pair of pincers, with which it dismembers its victims, and a long curving tail that ends in a poisonous sting. It is with the tail that it injects a venom that is, milligram for milligram, deadlier than snake venom. While the wound is not impressive, the sting actually goes deep, producing high fever, blurred vision and an adverse effect on both the nervous system and the heart. If it doesn't kill, the venom can cause a kind of insanity in the victim.

Legend has it that scorpions went out of their way to claim human victims. In one case related in tales, a bunch of them formed a chain from the ceiling to the face of a sleeping victim, and the last one on the chain made the bite. It is likely, however, that this is apocryphal because scorpions are not known to attack human beings. Hence, it also makes suspect a ninja's releasing a scorpion into the bedroom of a warlord and expecting it to attack without provocation.

While cyanide is thought of as a sophisticated, modern poison, it was commonly available for ninja of feudal times. They learned to extract it from various things such as the seeds of apples, apricots, cherries, plums and almonds; all of these are loaded with cyanide compounds which will have no effect on a person unless the compounds are given in large doses. One man, for example, was reputed to have saved a cupful of apple seeds —and then ate them all at once. He died within minutes.

In action, cyanide, taken orally, works on the central nervous system and kills very quickly. Ninja were usually partial to poisons which worked quickly, and it filled the bill quite nicely.

Some people might have been surprised to learn that the seeds of common fruit, as those mentioned above, were poisonous. They would probably be equally shocked to learn about the killing and/or paralyzing power of some other very common household plants and flowers. Ninja wouldn't be. They made it a point to know them well.

One deadly one is found in ordinary tomato leaves; not the tomato itself, of course, but the leaves. Eat these and you create cardiac problems and, ultimately, cardiac arrest.

Quite a few ninja enemies, it can be safely assumed, dined to death on tomato leaves. They could be simply slipped into a salad or the like and, unless one knew of their poisonous potency, they would look totally harmless and be fully ingested before one knew what hit him.

Another deadly tidbit for ninja enemies was rhubarb. That is the leaf blade, not the petiole, which can be safely eaten. The leaf contains oxalic acid, and once a little is eaten, it generates all manner of abdominal cramps. If a ninja enemy ate enough leaves he could easily slip into convulsions, coma and death.

Ninja were fond of serving to enemies the so-called death-cup mushroom, technically the *amanita phalloides*. This ordinary-looking mushroom is well deserving of its reputation as the most lethal mushroom in the world. One of the things ninja liked about it was that there was no antidote (a desirable quality in any poison). Once ingested and in the bloodstream that was it. The problem with the poison—from the point of view of those who had taken it—was that it actually consisted of a number of different poisons. One, for example, called phalloidin, is four times more powerful than cyanide; just fifty millionths of a gram will kill a mouse. Assuming the victim survives this, then there are three other poisons to deal with, such as amnitime, which is even more powerful than phalloidin, and others which work against the liver and kidneys.

While there is not any specific reference to it in the literature, ninja certainly must have used bamboo, which grows plentifully in Japan, as a poison. As noted in *National Geographic* magazine: "Many bamboos have culm sheaths covered with a down of fine hairs. Beware of touching these. They will get under the skin and produce intense irritation."

Indeed, this would have made an ideal poison. "Bacteria on the hairs could even cause blood poisoning. I had read," the author continues, "that in ancient times sheath hairs were mixed with food to get rid of an enemy."

Ninja did not always mean to kill an enemy. Sometimes the assignment involved using a poison just to paralyze, as mentioned, or cause blindness.

In one rather bizarre case two warlords were vying for control of a prefecture. One had announced to the other before a large assemblage of people that he was a God and had the power to strike anyone blind who stood in his way. The other warlord reacted derisively. Shortly after the dinner, however, the warlord indeed did go blind, and he announced to the world that the other warlord was a God.

Indeed. In fact it was a ninja—who had spiked

a bath towel of the shogun with poinsettia, which causes temporary blindness—who was the god-maker.

Sometimes poisons acted quickly, other times slowly . . . becoming, over a long period of time, cumulatively fatal. While a ninja normally didn't like this—he preferred a poison which would operate quickly in small amounts—slow poisoning could often be useful.

For example, there was a ninja who reputedly was a mole—an enemy agent living as an ordinary citizen in a town—who slowly but surely poisoned the "mayor" of that town over a period of months. The big advantage was that the ninja drank the same green tea in which he had slipped the poison, so that it calmed some suspicions the mayor had about the ninja. But ah! Each time after consuming the tea, the ninja had taken an antidote. Eventually, the mayor died a seemingly ordinary death, and the ninja was never suspected.

Another "poison" of feudal times, which ninja sometimes used, became known to American GI's during the war in Vietnam: Vietcong would dip their knives or spears in horse manure and blood. When the blade was used to cut, the blood/dung concoction would cause an infection that could kill.

Ninja of yesterday normally looked for a number of qualities or attributes in a poison. First would be one which worked fairly quickly (thus allowing them time to escape), one for which there was no antidote, one that didn't necessarily look like a poison in action. Today's ninja also wants those qualities in a poison and one other:

the poison can't be identified as such when an autopsy is done.

There are a variety of poisons like curare which fill this bill nicely. Even under the best conditions, and with a top-notch coroner, it is not as Simon-simple as TV and movies would have us believe to determine cause of death, no less come up with some microscopic tracings of a poison. There has been more than one such homicide, you can believe, which has appeared natural but has been the result of poison.

The delivery system is also, of course, much more sophisticated than it used to be. Ideally, a person will take the poison orally. But today, as mentioned in the chapter on weapons, there are needles which could be dipped in poison and which are so fine that it would be virtually impossible for a coroner to detect the entrance wound, particularly if the wound is made in an out-of-the-way spot.

While most of us think of poisons as being dramatic—like arsenic—ordinary household substances can be and have been used with deadly effect, and it has to be asumed by ninja so disposed. This would include not only material which is taken orally, but deadly gases formed by combining common household substances, such as the classic bleach with ammonia. More than one political or military personage has died in this way . . . and one wonders just how much of an accident their deaths were.

While not actually a poison, one other related modality of murder for ninja is the so-called Death Touch. As the name implies, the Death Touch is a way of touching someone to cause immediate or delayed death. Such a touch is often compared to poison because the relatively small amount of force used, as with poison, can deliver a lethal blow.

When the body is touched at certain times of the day, when the flow of blood or of the slight currents of electricity produced comes closest to the skin, the touch reportedly interrupts such a flow, causing death.

One may not touch just anywhere. There are certain points, called *atemi,* which must be contacted. A number of accounts state that the number of points is over 360 and while some must be touched, others must be grasped. Indeed, to do either the attacker must first memorize where they are, and this is part of some ninja's extensive knowledge of human anatomy.

The Death Touch kills slowly or instantly. It may produce an internal hemorrhage, which will cause a person to bleed to death, or produce a blood clot that will reach the heart hours, days or even months after the victim is touched; striking at other points of the body, it attacks the cardiovascular system with quicker results.

Chapter 8

EMPTY-HAND COMBAT

Empty-hand combat, fighting without a weapon, is as old as mankind itself. The first men must certainly have swung their arms, kicked their legs and butted with their heads when attacking or defending themselves against the attacks of other men or animals. But organized empty-hand fighting techniques didn't develop until man took those first steps toward being civilized . . . when he began to use basic tools and recognized that his arms and legs were also tools that could be developed and used more efficiently for combat.

There is no doubt that weaponless combat was practiced by all peoples in all parts of the world from the very beginning, but it was the Orientals who polished and perfected empty-hand techniques, learned to harness and control the powers of the arms and legs, making hand-to-hand combat a devastating art.

The ninja knew and studied hand-to-hand techniques, and he was undoubtedly very competent as an empty-hand fighter, even if he wasn't unusual. But to be competent in unarmed combat (like today's karate, kung fu, jujitsu men) is shockingly formidable. A well-trained karate black belt can easily punch through three one-inch boards or snap a brick in two with a sharp *shuto* ("knife-hand strike"). But to some dedicated martial artists, these remarkable feats seem like child's play.

George Dillman of Reading, Pennsylvania, for example, has shattered a thousand pounds of ice (ten one-hundred-pound blocks piled one atop the other) with a single smash of his forearm. The mountain of ice was so high he had to stand on a chair to do it. And there are others who have learned to generate enough speed and power to break ten two-inch cinderblocks with a driving punch and, in a few cases, by striking with their foreheads. Other masters of breaking can snap five inches of wood with a front or side kick (with the toes or ball or outer blade of the foot). Imagine, then, what any of these men are capable of doing to the human body.

It is not unusual for a karateka to deliver multiple punches, as many as four, in the space of a second. Film star Chuck Norris, when he was an active karate champion, demonstrated this ability on many occasions at seminars. And the great Bill Wallace, who recently retired as the undefeated Professional Karate Association's full-contact Middleweight Champion could easily deliver three well-focused kicks—kicks that are not merely flicks of the foot, but capable of doing severe damage—in the space of one second There's no wonder that his nickname is "Superfoot."

We can be sure that the ninja, trained in empty-hand techniques (even if they weren't as

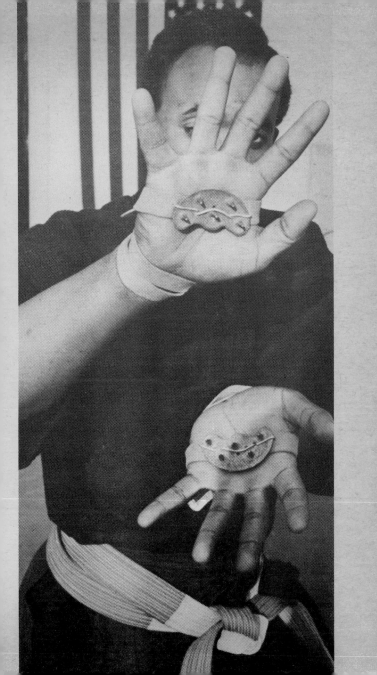

Dr. Masaaki Hatsumi, the 34th Supreme Master of Togakure Ryu ninjutsu.

Steve Hayes, American ninja.

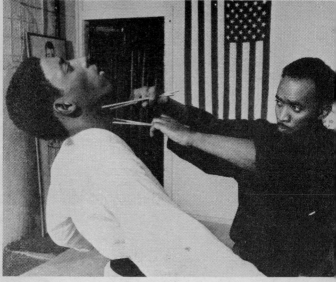

Ron Duncan shows how everyday chopsticks can be turned into a formidable weapon.

In his film, *Octagon,* from American Cinema
Productions, Chuck Norris as "James Scott" battles
Kyo, a ninja warrior. Kyo's uniform and weapons (the
Okinawan *sai*) would be considered unorthodox by ninja
of the past.

NINJA EQUIPMENT

Foot Spikes: Laced across the foot, they provide extra grip for climbing and scaling.

Calthrops (Tetsu-Bishi): Metal spikes constructed so that one point is always up. Used on the ground to stop warriors on foot, but can also be thrown.

Shuriken: These come in all sizes, weights and shapes. The four-pointed one is closest to the classical *shuriken*.

NINJA EQUIPMENT

Climbing Claws: Modern, authentically styled claw slips over hands. Can also be used as a fighting weapon.

Shuriken Cases: This pack stores *shurikens* and attaches to belt. It is a modern version of the pouch carried by the ninja.

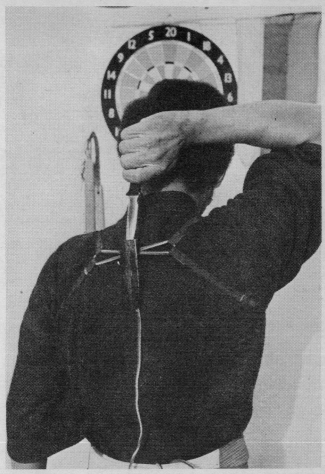

Joe Griffith

A weapon for the modern ninja...a throwing knife in a sheath strapped to the back, easily accessible and, in Ron Duncan's hands, extremely deadly.

Stalking, camouflage and defenses against the knife are all part of the traditional training of the ninja that Steve Hayes keeps alive.

Christopher J. McLoughlin

Joe Griffith

The *manriki gusari,* a short chain (usually two or three feet) with weighted ends. It can be used as a garrote, to tie a man up or block his blow, or swung so the weighted ends make contact.

Manriki: Modern versions of the tool used by ninja to strike and trap. The weighted ends are lethal weapons, and the chain can also be used to choke or, wrapped around an arm or leg, hold a victim.

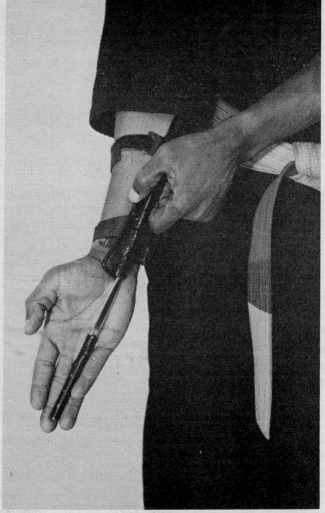

Joe Griffith

A dagger in a sheath strapped to the forearm (usually hidden by the sleeve of a coat) can be in the hand and ready for action with a flick of the wrist.

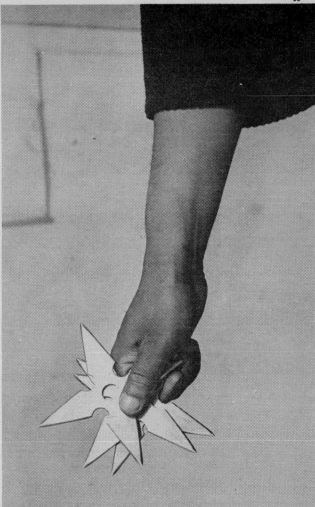

Joe Griffith

Ron Duncan, ready to go into action with three
shuriken, the deadly throwing stars. These weapons are
particularly potent when the sharp points are coated with
poison.

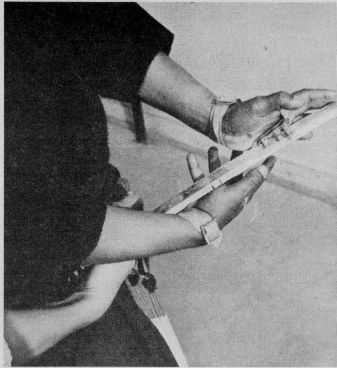

The *shuko* ("tiger claws"), which are used for climbing trees and scaling castle walls, can also be used to trap and parry a sword.

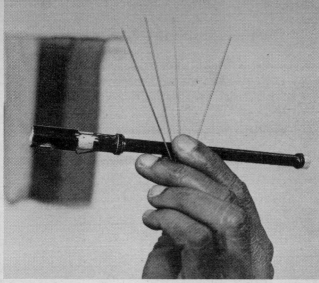

A small, easily hidden blowgun with the needlelike darts that can be coated with poison. A favorite weapon of the ninja.

Joe Griffith

Steve Hayes uses the *manriki* to trap the arm of an "enemy."

Unarmed combat is an integral part of ninja training. Today's ninja borrows heavily from other martial arts. Here Hayes (left) and student Larry Beaver assume their ready positions (1). As Beaver steps in and throws an overhand right punch, Hayes

1

2

3

4

counters, in the ninja tradition, with a strike/ block to the underside of the attacker's arm (2). The block stops the blow but also does a fair amount of damage to the arm. Hayes then brings his left hand to a high position, guarding his face (unlike the traditional return to chamber in karate), and throws a right counter-punch (reverse punch) to the jaw (3) and then steps in and behind the right foot of Beaver to perform an arm lock that will bring Larry to the ground (4).

Christopher J. McLoughlin

Steve Hayes employs the *kusarigama* against opponents armed with sword and bow. Deftly trapping the sword-bearer's hands with the weighted chain, Hayes pulls him off balance (1,2). While shifting to the side, he uses the attacker's body to run interference while further checking against a last-breath side slash with the sword. The finishing touch is a throat slash with the sickle end of his weapon (3). As the second man begins his attack, Hayes uses his weapon now as a blocking instrument (4), then takes firm hold of the *bo* and pulls quickly while delivering a front kick to the attacker's groin (5).

Christopher J. McLoughlin

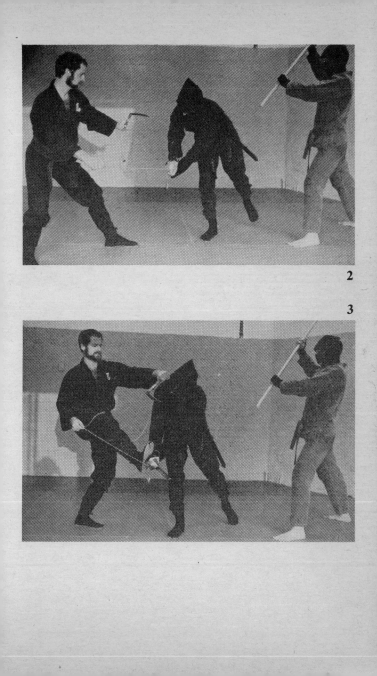

4

5

1

Bo and *Jo* stick techniques not only enable the ninja to block and strike, but expand the useful possibilities to trapping (1) and body maneuvering for the delivery of an unexpected technique, like a knee to the midsection (2).

2

perfected as they are today) could easily kill with his hands and feet. He was taught where the best spots to hit were. And he hit hard.

Ninja knew how and where to hit and how and where to apply pressures to paralyze or kill an opponent. The ninja, like the Chinese whose arts of fighting he adopted, was well versed in the anatomy of the body. He knew most, if not all, of the spots where pressure or a blow could be applied to stop or disable an enemy. He knew that if he struck the ears of a man with cupped hands, he would build up enough pressure to shatter the eardrum and destroy the delicate mechanism of the inner ear. This would, at least, cause excruciating pain . . . at best, it could send a man into a state of shock or kill him.

He knew that if he applied pressure to certain areas under the jaw, he could immobilize a man, and by moving his fingers a few inches to another part of the neck, he could bring on unconsciousness.

The ninja, as a trained empty-hand fighter, knew then and knows now what area of the body to strike with what technique to cause the most damage. He knows, for example, that the thumb can be very effective when striking the temple or ear. The spear hand (striking with the extended, tightened tips of the fingers) can be deadly, when directed with full power, to the eyes, throat, pit of the stomach or abdomen. The knife hand (*shuto*) is a fine technique to use against the face, collarbone or kidneys. In fact, the *shuto,* used by a trained martial artist, can break the neck of an opponent.

The foot, which can generate much more power than the hands when used by the trained martial artist, turns the weaponless fighter into a veritable war-machine. The front kick, thrust or snapped out forward with upturned toes and the ball of the foot generally used for striking, aimed at the stomach or groin, can take all the fight out of a man. And a side kick (the weapon is the blade of the foot) can shatter a knee joint or rib with relative ease. A roundhouse kick, brought up and around so the fighter strikes with the instep of his foot, can collapse a cheekbone or fracture a skull.

It is safe to say that none of these techniques would be any more than street-fight punches and kicks if they weren't built on the foundation of "focus" (*kime*), which is the ability of the trained martial artist to concentrate all his energy, both physical and mental, for that moment when he strikes the target. Through constant practice and study, he is able to develop the proper balance between speed and power, add it to the right body alignment, combine it with strong mental concentration, and then the blow he delivers becomes deadly. One further factor is important: proper breath control. At the exact moment of contact, the breath should be exhaled sharply. That's one reason for the loud scream (*kiai*) we hear martial artists use when they attack.

The hand and foot are not the only weapons of the arm and leg. The forearm smash is particularly effective. The same is true of the knee and elbow. When grappling with an opponent, full kicks and punches are not possible. These in-close techniques, when used by a man or woman who has studied and perfected them, can inflict a great deal of punishment.

We must also remember that a fighter can't be trained only in aggressive techniques if he hopes to be successful. He must also be capable of presenting a strong, impregnable defense. A man who can throw a solid punch or kick but can't block the attack of his opponent could easily find himself down for the count. In the case of the ninja, this count could be the last he would ever hear.

A good defense, if properly executed, can prove to be an effective offense. The ninja who blocks the punch of an attacker by striking at the inside of the forearm, close to the elbow, with a round swinging knuckle smash not only stops the blow but also does enough damage so that his opponent will hesitate before using that technique again. If the block is fully effective, the ninja will have the chance to move in with an attack of his own before his adversary can recover.

A strong, often disabling defense can be used against kick attacks as well. The ninja, up against a fighter who goes on the offensive with a front kick to the groin, parries the technique with a kick of his own, usually directed at the knee, the hamstring muscle above and behind the knee or the sensitive muscles just below and behind the knee. Obviously, this takes a great deal of practice and perfect timing. The attacking leg must be met when it is in the proper position so that these sensitive areas can be reached by the defender's kick. Anyone who has ever pulled a hamstring muscle or has suffered an injury to his knee can easily imagine how disabling powerful blows to these areas can be.

The empty-hand block can also be effective against an attacker with a weapon. Of course, using the naked arm to stop the slash of a sharp sword would be an obvious mistake, but the ninja

could stop the thrusts or slashes of a *bo* (staff)
or spear without the aid of a weapon. Again we
see the need for extensive training—a complete
mastery of body alignment, speed and timing. If,
for example, a spear-bearing warrior attacked by
thrusting his weapon at the midsection of the
ninja, the intended victim could parry the thrust
with what is commonly called an outside forearm
block. When the spear reached the proper position,
the ninja would strike it a short distance from its
point by swinging his forearm (arm bent at the
elbow, fist pointed upward at head level) from the
outside to about the center of his body. At the
completion of the block, his elbow would end up
at the middle of his chest, about six inches in
front of his body; his fist would be at eye level,
the palm side toward his face.

The ninja also had to be capable of fighting
from the ground. If he were to trip or be taken off
his feet by an attacker, he had to be ready to
defend himself from a prone position. When
seemingly the most vulnerable, he had to keep
his wits about him and fight with the same cunning he would use if he were still on his feet.

When flat on his back and apparently defenseless, he could use his feet to kick at the knee or
groin or to trap the leg of his opponent and bring
him down. This could be accomplished by placing
the instep of one foot behind his attacker's ankle
and the lower part of his other leg to the side of
his opponent's knee. Pushing at the knee while
simultaneously pulling at the ankle, he could break
his opponent's balance and make him fall flat on
his back. Keeping the leg trapped and locked with
his own, he could then disable his attacker with

fist strikes to his spine or a *shuto* to the back of his neck.

A variation of this takedown that is also effective is to hook one foot behind the ankle and pull as you deliver a strong side kick to the midsection.

When the ninja was down, he was by no means out. He was still a cunning, dangerous fighter.

To know the empty-hand fighting techniques of the ninja, we merely have to examine the techniques taught by the Togakure Ryu, which are called *taijutsu*.

It is fascinating to think that some aspects of the *taijutsu* (it has been revised down through the years) which this modern *ryu* practices have been passed down through thirty-four generations. It is a blend of the physical and the philosophical.

On the physical side, *taijutsu* consists of *kamae*, or postures, "that reflect the fighting attitude," as the Togakure combat manual says. The *kamae* are not static but are adjusted to meet the particular fighting attitude of the opponent. There is the *hira kamae*, natural posture—hands on hips, feet apart; the defensive posture—*inchimonji kamae*—sort of like an open boxer's stance but with the extended or leading hand open, weight on the rear leg, waiting for the attack and ready to respond, and the *jumomji kamae*, the offensive posture, which is not unlike the boxer's stance, the arms in close, hands near the face, body slightly forward with the weight on the front leg so the fighter is ready to move in.

From these basic postures the fledgling ninja is taught how to punch (*tsuki*) with a ninja fist (a regular fist except the thumb nail is pressed down on top of the knuckle of the forefinger). There is also *keri* or kicking, which is designed to deliver smashing blows, not ones "snapped or flicked into place and quickly withdrawn," or to unbalance an opponent.

Shuto, or open-hand strikes, are also taught. In one version the fist is swung at the opponent, but the hand is snapped open at the moment of contact for maximum impact. Open-hand strikes, making impact with the points of the fingers, are also used against soft targets like stomach, throat or eyes.

One nasty but effective way of disabling an opponent with an open hand is striking with the heel of the palm (palm-heel strike) to the base of the nose. The rising strike, if powerfully executed, is capable of driving the cartilage of the nose into the brain. Even if it isn't that lethal, it is certainly sure to put an opponent out of action.

The palm-heel strike is particularly effective when applied to the head, but it can also do a great deal of damage when delivered to the area of the body just below the sternum. This blow can be delivered quickly, with little preparation and, therefore, very little warning to an opponent.

Ninja would sometimes engage in empty-hand combat in the water, and so he developed a few techniques for fighting there. In the Togakure Ryu system, for example, the combat manual details the location of the windpipe so that a pair of fingers will stop air flow and incapacitate the fighter.

Another technique works well if you want to drive an attacker away. Just jam the thumbs of your balled-up fists under and into the ribs below the pectoral muscles and push—it works quite well.

If someone is gripping the ninja, a good technique for making the grip relax is to apply pinching pressure to the forearm below the elbow. This effectively weakens an attacker's hold.

For forcing an attacker downward, the technique is to hook the fingers over the collarbone and dig down behind it. A downward pressure will effectively take the man to the ground.

Though it is true that we don't know a great deal about the techniques used by the early ninja because of their penchant for secrecy, it is safe to say that their empty-hand fighting styles came from the same source as those of other Oriental martial artists. But because they had to learn so many other skills, we can assume they didn't develop as wide a repertoire as those martial artists who devoted all their time to empty-hand training and fighting. And because the ninja is one who adopts and adapts, we know that, today, he would have a working knowledge of all the present-day styles, using techniques from karate, kung fu, t'ai chi ch'uan, tae kwon do and the others.

The fighting arts as we know them today (the Oriental arts, that is) were brought to China from India by the monk Bodhidharma, who instructed the priests in both the mental and physical disciplines that he had developed. The Chinese converted the Indian fighting method into Chinese *Kempo,* a style more suited to their culture. This fighting system, practiced only by priests, quickly spread through China, eventually being taught to the general population to help them protect themselves against thieves and bandits. Simultaneously, in the mountains of China, a fist-fighting technique was developed by a man named To-san-fen. This became known as *wu-tang-shan* (*butosan* in Japanese) *kempo* and involved the study of five elements: the soul, the emotions, bravery, strength and the body.

These systems moved on to Korea, where they were again adjusted to fit the character and culture of the people. And they also moved on to Japan to become the foundation of the Japanese martial arts. Of course, the Japanese had some form of martial arts from the moment the first inhabitant raised a stick or hand in anger, but it was from the Chinese (and Koreans) that they learned the refinements, the studied, proven techniques that shaped the martial arts in Japan during the heyday of the ninja up to modern times.

The ninja today is undoubtedly a much better empty-hand fighter than his ancestor was. He is the beneficiary of the refinements that have taken place over the years in the martial arts and, because of better communications and the increased interaction between peoples, he has been exposed to the many styles that exist in the world today. He is in the position to choose the best of each and can now become a far more formidable and fearsome fighter than ever before. His ancestor was not so lucky. The ancient ninja lived in a closed society. His exposure to new ways of fighting was limited. He did extremely well with what was available to him. But he never had the opportunities his heirs have.

The medieval ninja certainly knew both grappling and striking techniques, but they were taught and practiced as two separate and distinct styles and rarely combined. Today, the ninja knows the two can be quite effective when combined. A grab, sweep and punch is far better and much more disabling than just a grab; a punch, sweep and stomp can do much more damage than just a punch. Though the ancient techniques are still very valid, the new additions and refinements make them that much more lethal.

The drive to "win" is strong in all of us, but we are prevented, in many cases, from coming out on top in a fight because of inhibitions that control us (conscious or unconscious) that have been instilled in us by our culture. Kick a man in the groin? Outrageous, unsportsmanlike. Gouge out a man's eye? Not on your life. But the ninja has no such inhibitions. The code he would follow in an all-out fight is governed by his drive to win, to succeed, to survive.

"Placed in a situation where my survival was at stake," says Ron Duncan, "and without weapons of any sort to help me, I would come up with and use any technique I could that would disable my opponent. And I wouldn't worry about sportsmanship. That's for competing athletes, not for ninja."

To help him in a life-or-death situation, Ron can draw from the many styles of martial arts he has studied. As a trained jujitsuan, he can make devastating use of the locks, twists, throws and strikes that style teaches, or he can use his knowledge of *isshin-ryu* (the Okinawan style of karate developed by Master Tatsuo Shimabuku) that features powerful, lightning-fast blows that helped weaponless Okinawans defeat armed Japanese invaders.

But empty-hand ninja of today would also use many of the same methods used by the early ninja. He would strike with fingers and fists (and kicks) to those areas that are most sensitive or vulnerable. He would strike or apply pressure to the nerve areas of the neck and arms that are least protected to control or disable an opponent. He would use spit, sand or dust to temporarily blind an adversary. He would bite, claw and stab with his nails. He would pop out an eyeball with his fingers or tear the testicles from a man with a viselike grip. He would chop, punch and kick joints until they broke. He would, in short, be considered a "dirty" fighter . . . but he would survive, and more than likely, he would win.

Although there are tales of feats of empty-hand martial artists that are gross exaggerations or out-and-out lies, no one who has even a passing knowledge of the Oriental fighting arts will ever deny the great strength and power a weaponless fighter can develop if he is properly trained . . . if he has a thorough understanding of his body's capabilities and has mastered the power of *ki,* the inner strength. The ninja did (and does) know his capabilities and did develop *ki.*

How much power can the trained martial artist muster? We presented illustrations of bricks and cinderblocks being destroyed by a single blow and mountains of ice collapsing under the strike of an elbow. These have all been shown publicly at martial arts events and on TV. But what of the other feats, less well known?

Masutatsu (Mas) Oyama, one of the most famous of recent karateka and the author of one of the "bibles" of the martial artist, *This Is Karate,* secluded himself in the mountains of Japan for three years developing his physical and mental resources and could finally smash trees and stones with his bare hands. When he returned to civilization, he demonstrated the powers he had developed by tearing the horns from charging bulls. It was also reported that he killed bulls with a single punch to the head.

Other martial artists have broken iron bars with *shuto* strikes and have hammered nails through wood with their fists. One New York *sensei*, attacked on the streets by three would-be muggers, disabled two and killed the third with a single punch to the head. The punch caused multiple fractures. The skull just shattered.

The story is told of one ninja who so developed the power of his right leg, he could literally kick through bodies. In a fight against an armed warrior, he delivered a kick to the groin that tore off the man's testicles and buried his toes into the soldier's lower intestine.

The development of *ki* not only helps the ninja deliver a powerful blow, but also builds in him the power to take one. By mustering his inner strength, he can withstand withering attacks that would destroy other men. He has complete mastery of his body and can "turn off" pain and build a shield that will protect him from injury. Ninja of the past could withstand brutal torture and not show any sign of pain. They would not cry out, often frustrating their torturers, and would die seemingly oblivious to the brutality being inflicted upon them.

A modern example of this great power of inner strength is a martial artist named Frank DeFelice. He has publicly allowed other powerful karateka to beat him with punches and kicks delivered with all the force they could muster. They have not yet been able to knock him down or hurt him. And they have kicked and punched him in the throat and groin.

An offshoot of this power of *ki* is the *kiai* or
"spirit shout" used by ninja as well as other martial artists in empty-hand fighting. It is a natural
release of breath and noise that accompanies the
expending of physical and mental energy. The
Togakure masters compare the sounds ninja make
to dogs growling and barking while fighting, or
the yell used at the moment of lifting something
heavy, such as weightlifters use.

The *kiai* are nonspecific—sounds that are not
words but rather reactions to situations. There are
four situations to which a ninja of the Togakure
Ryu is expected to respond.

One is the "attacking shout," a kind of rebel
yell that the ninja whoops at the moment of attack. It is designed to startle or stun the opponent
for just a moment; and in the accelerated world
of unarmed combat, a moment is all that is required.

Another is the "victorious shout," a kind of
"yahhh" that the opponent is supposed to hear
and be demoralized by. As with the attacking
shout, it helps produce greater power by adding
inner strength to the physical blow.

The shout of "discovery or enlightenment" is
"similar to a detective's exclamation" upon finding
an important clue. But the clue in this case would
be the method or pattern of fighting which an opponent has been using which the ninja has discovered. This can also be somewhat demoralizing
when an opponent realizes the ninja knows and
can handle whatever he can deliver.

Finally, there is the internal shout of "silent
kiai"—a "low rumbling growl" . . . of vibrations
so low in pitch that they are inaudible. This is the

highest form of *kiai,* and would sound similar to "ah-unri" if it was audible.

As mentioned earlier, there was a philosophical aspect of empty-hand combat, as there was in other aspects of a ninja's activity. This philosophy for the Togakure Ryu and how empty-hand combat fits in is explained by Steve Hayes in Chapter Ten.

Chapter 9

INVISIBILITY

In the feudal period of Japan, the very thought of a ninja was enough to make a man tremble. People didn't think of them as human, but rather as superhuman—as animals (one popular view was as a *tengo,* half man, half crow) who could perform incredible feats of running, leaping, climbing.

Above all, though, people thought of ninja as being able to make themselves invisible.

This is partly because of the ninja's reputation for covert penetration of a defense and escape. The literature on ninja is filled with stories about warlords and other high-ranking officials who were murdered—clearly by ninja—with no trace of the ninja's presence. There are many stories, too, about the dramatic and unexplainable escapes ninja were capable of. In one early text, for example, a ninja was being pursued to the edge of a cliff. There was no way back and no way down. To escape, he must fly. And, of course, he did.

The methods ninja used to accomplish their

goals contribute to an understanding of what is meant by "invisible."

The ninja himself did not want a direct confrontation with an enemy because he was invariably outnumbered. If he could perform his job without being seen, his chances for success and survival were so much the better.

The night was normally the best time for the ninja, especially if the weather was very bad. A rain or snowstorm would not only reduce visibility, but samurai guards were less likely to be alert.

In his approach, besides being difficult to see, the ninja would be difficult, if not impossible, to hear. He was trained to control his breathing and to tread lightly.

In addition to stealth, ninja were also trained in the art of hiding. In *do-ton jutsu,* or earth techniques, they learned how to secrete themselves or their gear among rocks or uneven ground. For example, ninja could shape their bodies like natural or manmade objects, such as boulders or statues, so that they were undetectable in the darkness.

Moku-ton jutsu, wood and plant techniques, involved hiding in trees and foliage or tall grass. Ninja were taught how to lie in tall grass so it did not move or appear unnatural under the scrutiny of an enemy.

Ninja would also frequently hide themselves in the ground, burying themselves completely except for their bamboo snorkels. It undoubtedly made an effective and unpleasant surprise for a guard to be walking along and suddenly to see the ground in front of him bulge and break and yield up a black-suited ninja bent on killing him.

Ninja also made a science of house construction. Some of the homes and fortresses of Japan's feudal age were built of stone, but many were wood—and a labyrinth of wood, at that—all warrened with false ceilings and floors and secret passages and closets.

Depending on the rank of the individual ninja and the size of the *ryu* he was a member of, his house would be simple or elaborate. The more elaborate, the greater the variety of things built into it which would affect his escape.

A standard item would be a trapdoor, and it would invariably lead to a tunnel that let the ninja emerge in a spot that was unlikely to be covered by an enemy.

False ceilings were also used. The ceiling would appear to be more shallow than it was, and someone searching for a ninja would immediately dismiss it as a potential hiding place.

Floors, too, were hid beneath, often right under the front entrance—the foyer or vestibule area of the house. The ninja was well aware that a searcher would probably penetrate more deeply into the house rather than search near the entryway.

Many ninja houses had attics, and these were also utilized as hiding places, as long as the hiding place was not obvious. If the ninja could secrete himself between, say, a pair of rafters and be covered by a removable panel of ceiling material, that would be suitable.

The ninja, because of his physical condition, could also hide in spots that would seem difficult, if not impossible, for most people. But limber muscles and the ability to dislocate joints enabled the ninja to do it.

As with all things, the ninja exercised deception

even within the context of escape mechanisms built into his home.

For example, he would make it appear that he had taken a particular escape route when he had not by leaving a slightly misaligned mat over a trapdoor. A searcher would peel back the mat, open the trapdoor, see the tunnel and naturally assume that the ninja had escaped that way. Meanwhile, the ninja would be hiding in the ceiling of the adjacent room.

Ninja appreciated the value of surprise and had a decided aversion to being surprised themselves. To guard against this they fashioned their own primitive but highly efficient security systems.

These could range from simple bells on entry doors to perimeter systems. One of the latter, for example, consisted of black thread strung like a small fence around the ninja's property. The lines were linked to bells inside the house that would tinkle when someone walked into them. The ninja would know he was about to have an unwelcome visitor.

Dogs were sometimes used and ninja also learned to "read" the more subtle changes in the sounds made by creatures in the area around his home, like crickets, when their environment was disturbed. No one, not even another ninja, could slip by undetected.

Knowledge of house construction and security measures would help a ninja anticipate and prepare for situations he might encounter on a mission. He could determine fairly accurately what he would find once inside a house, and he undoubtedly had spies working for him who would provide information about the layout.

This knowledge was often a lifesaver, since it

allowed the ninja to plan his escape route before-hand.

Sometimes the escape would have to be made slowly. There are stories about ninja who killed warlords, then purposely hid in false ceilings or closets *in the room* with the deceased, rightly figuring that the samurai would search every place else. Later, when things calmed down, they stole away. Such action took great coolness, a quality which ninja had in excess.

Sometimes this self-possession—and a ninja's ability to stay absolutely quiet—was put to an extreme test.

In 1478, a ninja named Yamoto was assigned the task of killing a high-ranking samurai named Herrito. The ninja's plan was to penetrate the house and the samurai's bedroom, hide in the beams, then lower himself in the middle of the night and kill the sleeping man.

The ninja got into the room and into the ceiling beams, but the samurai came into the room with two other warriors and they played *go* at a table not six feet from where the ninja was hiding. They played for five hours, and the ninja had to remain absolutely motionless and silent during that entire time. He did, plus another hour, finally emerging when the samurai was asleep and killing him.

This remarkable ability to hide is shared by feudal as well as modern ninja. A former marine captain described an astonishing feat from World War II. "It was learned," he says, "that a ninja could hide in a completely bare room! Where? Braced up in the corner near the ceiling, on either the left or right side of the doorway. When someone came into the room their peripheral vision wouldn't pick out the ninja!"

While a ninja would often slink into a place by stealth, he might also do it under cover of a diversion. The most simple way was to toss a stone or branch in one direction while heading in the other. A variation would to be to release an animal, or perhaps more than one, like a few rats, or a snake, or a dog, to divert a guard's attention.

Another maneuver would be to launch an attack with ten or twenty men at one end of a compound while a single ninja slipped in at the other. Similarly, by firing a flaming arrow into a building, the ninja could slip in while everyone was occupied with putting the fire out.

Ninja would also disguise themselves as priests, teachers, peasants or even samurai in order to get into or out of a place. Also, they might ride under a load of something in a wagon.

Ninja planned their escape routes very carefully, usually with a built-in contingency strategy.

For example, a ninja was hotly pursued by samurai through fields when he suddenly disappeared. He had jumped into a hole which had already been dug, and pulled the prepared camouflage over himself.

The ninja would do what was unexpected. An important aspect of his training, the art of *kyojutsu ten kan ho,* taught him to prepare an enemy to think in one way and then surprise him by doing something else.

An illustration is the case of a ninja pursued into an open field where there was tall grass and only a few, unclimbable trees. The ninja would have left a rope hanging down from the lowest branch on one of the trees, and he would quickly hoist himself up. Meanwhile, his pursuers would be looking for him among the grasses.

Ninja were skilled at operating in, around and under water. In the Togakure Ryu *sui-ton jutsu* or water techniques of escape were practiced. They had a variety of equipment to use, from rafts to water spiders and snorkels.

While ninja were famous for their physical disappearing acts, there was another type of invisibility called *hensu jutsu*. This involves the ninja's blending with, becoming part of, the fabric of a community . . . and learning vital espionage information over several years. Such an action indicates the deep level of commitment expected from a ninja because it required sometimes devoting his entire life behind enemy lines, sacrificing all for the cause.

As with other aspects of ninjutsu, each *ryu* had its own techniques for training its deep-cover spies. For the Togakure Ryu there were "seven ways of going," or *shichi ho do* . . . seven disguises that were favored: "wandering monk, mountain warrior, entertainer, farmer or farmworker, a traveling priest and soldier for hire," as Steve Hayes's "Ninja Combat Method" points out.

Because some of the disguises would be inappropriate for the modern ninja, the masters of today's Togakure Ryu system concocted some substitutes, but still retain seven ways of being inconspicuous. Hayes recalls entering a room in Japan knowing there were ninja present, but he had no idea who they were. They blended in perfectly with the others present.

Ninja are able to do this by exercising complete and constant control over their emotions, appearance and mannerisms. They make sure they never overact or underact; they never overdress or underdress. They have learned to blend quickly into an environment, no matter how foreign it may be to them. When they dress, they choose clothes that are perfectly suitable for the occasion; when they speak, their voices are properly modulated—never too soft, never too loud. When they walk, they assume the speed of those around them. Their movements are never abrupt. In short, they train very hard so they will go unnoticed. They become invisible.

The ways of the Togakure Ryu are:

ENTERTAINER. This could include actors, singers, musicians, sports figures, reporters or models. In typical ninja fashion, the masters pay attention to devious detail and caution that the ninja should concentrate on things that would affect the ninja looking as if he belonged.

Some obvious considerations would be that sports figures have appropriate physiques, models should have a portfolio, musicians should be able to perform, and actors should have a résumé with pictures.

SCHOLAR. This category would include students, writers, artists, teachers and could also include radical types. A student or teacher would have a campus or intellectual area with which he is familiar. An artist or writer would be able to create, or at least be able to display someone else's work as his own creation. Radicals would have some core of belief of movement with which to identify.

RELIGIOUS. This narrow classification could include priests, rabbis, evangelists and even some types of social workers. It might be noted, the manual points out, that religious personages are often given special respect by society, even by those persons not believing in the particular religion being presented. Obviously, any ninja posing as a religious figure would have to have knowledge of the religion assumed.

The religious category was a favorite of ninja of past times. One reads numerous stories of their blending into a community as respected priests. Sometimes their true identities would be discovered, but there are cases of ninja priests living their entire lives in a particular community.

RURAL. Under this heading ninja of Togakure Ryu placed farmers, ranchers, woodsmen and any personality types identified with a rural or country setting. Farmers should have specific crops or livestock with which they dealt. Ranchers should be competent on horseback and have a knowledge of animals. Woodsmen should be aware of hunting season dates, appropriate caliber weapons for specific game and should possess suitable gear and equipment. It should be remembered that the smaller the town, the more difficult it would be fitting into the community anonymously.

BUSINESS. This is a very broad category which ranges in scope from salesmen and merchants to office workers and secretaries. The basic uniting factor in this classification is business attire and grooming, and it might be noted that "business" is one of the most easily assumed identities. Business cards and stationery can be printed inexpensively, and basic business skills are easily attainable.

LABORER. Another broad classification of identity, this would include construction workers, painters, gardeners, truck drivers or any other similar occupations of self-employed nature in which one uses physical skills. Another easily assumed identity, the laborer is often identified simply by paint-spattered clothes, a carpenter's tool belt or a sun tan and grass clippings on the trousers.

MAINTENANCE. This would include repairmen, meter readers, mechanics, janitors and merchant police or security guards. The uniting factor in this category would be some sort of uniform worn and the assumption of passersby that the ninja in the assumed identity is supposed to be there, whether he is taking apart an air-conditioning unit or directing traffic.

To make any of the above identities work, the masters advise that the ninja should "bear in mind several important considerations. . . ."

On appearance, they caution that the ninja should pick an identity that he or she fits into readily. Proper age is important—makeup and the like should not be relied on. "Hairstyles are of crucial importance. . . . Be sure that the length and combing direction of your hair fit the character assumed.

"Skin texture and coloring are also important, especially of the hands." They should meld with the identity. And, of course, careful dressing will be important.

Essential to success is knowledge of the profession or job. The ninja is counseled to absorb knowledge also "either in terms of intellectual facts or physical skill. . . . Therefore, it is wise to adopt a background with which you have a natural tie, as details can be deadly to the unsure." The masters also suggest that the ninja should have a good working knowledge of the area and public transportation.

Voice quality and language are also something

the modern-day ninja, just as his forebears, is taught to observe carefully. If he is assuming a role in a country or area which is foreign to him, he is cautioned to keep his speaking to a bare minimum unless he is well versed in the dialect and accent of the area. "Ninja will use as few words as possible," the manual says, realizing that the more he says, the greater the chance of the listener detecting a mistake in details.

In addition to the men, women and children also practiced *henso jutsu*.

In terms of hiding their identities as ninja, women agents *(kunoichi)* were particularly suited, especially if they were pretty.

Women were used mainly as intelligence gatherers, feudal-age Mata Haris. A man, or men, particularly in those days when chauvinism was rampant, was much more likely to let his guard down in front of a woman than he would in front of a man. So, ninja women were often the beneficiaries of stray bits of intelligence that a man would never have heard.

A female ninja's not-so-secret weapon was her sex appeal. It formed a natural smokescreen concealing her real purpose. It would be difficult, indeed, for a warlord smitten with a woman's beauty to think that behind those liquid eyes was a ninja mind registering everything that might be militarily important.

Some *ryus* specialized in supplying female agents, and such agents would be trained in most of the courses studied by men. For example, one *ryu* would supply an agent for espionage activities, another for assassination.

There is evidence that ninja woman did indeed kill. A favorite method, as mentioned elsewhere, was for the woman to stab the victim with a poison pin secreted in a bouffant hairstyle.

If gathering intelligence, or assassination, or whatever the desired end happened to be, sexual favors worked well. Ninja knew that a man would say things in the privacy of a bedroom that he wouldn't dream of saying elsewhere. To elicit information *kunoichi* were trained to compliment men on their virility and importance. The tendency of a man, usually, was to respond with material —such as military secrets—to prove just how important he was.

Like men, ninja women underwent physical training, though it was not usually as structured or intense. Still, women were trained in hand-to-hand combat and the use of the knife.

The hand-to-hand training was particularly difficult because it was felt, quite rightly by the *jonin* who designed the training courses, that a woman would be fighting a man rather than a woman. As such, they fought men in their courses—and hard. There was more than one case in which the bones of a woman were broken in hand-to-hand training ... and the same thing happened to men.

Not only ninja women would fight men. During the four hundred years of civil strife, the wife of a samurai developed into quite an ally of her husband, and a formidable ally at that. Many were trained in the use of such specialized weapons as the *naginata,* which was a staff six or seven feet long with a razor-sharp two-foot curved knife attached, and the *kusarigama,* the scythe or sickle and chain which the male ninja used so effectively. They could also fight with the *tessena,* a kind of iron fan.

Like the samurai men, the women also were

fanatics when it came to the ~~concept of death before dishonor~~. ~~The men would take their own lives~~
by *seppuku* ~~or belly slitting, while the women~~
~~would also kill themselves with their own~~ special
form of suicide called *jigai*, or throat cutting.

Indeed, samurai women were so dedicated to
the cause that they were known to kill blood relatives—father, son, brother, sister—if the person
had dishonored him or herself, or were supposed to
commit *seppuku* and could not. Such women
would also kill their own children if their capture
was imminent; the enemies in those days took de-
light in torturing the young as a means of terrifying their elders.

It was bad enough for a ninja to be captured.
The tortures were exquisite, and included stripping
the skin from the ninja's body, boiling him alive
in oil or water, or slowly breaking every bone in
his body. When a *kunoichi* was captured the
agony was extreme. Indeed, one historian of the
period remarked that "multiple rape would only
be the first in a series of agonies (she) would
have to endure."

There is evidence that children, also, acted as
spies. A ninja child, perhaps like his counterpart
in Vietnam, was fully capable of killing as well
as gathering intelligence. He might have had child-
ish notions, but they were ultimately made sub-
servient to his duty as a ninja.

The invisibility of women and children, their
acting as spies, was more surprising than a man's
doing it. You might expect a man to do such
things, but a woman was not generally regarded as
a *bushi* in any way, nor was a child. But as many an
enemy learned, it was an image that could be dan-
gerously and sometimes disastrously misleading.

Chapter 10

STEVE HAYES,
AMERICAN NINJA

When you think of a ninja, what comes to mind? If you're like most people who have seen some of the more recent martial arts films or read some of the latest novels that present ninja in action, your mind will conjure up a sinister figure, dressed in black from head to toe, a phantom in the shadows, and no doubt on a clandestine mission that will end with lots of blood and gore.

Your time reference may place your ninja in feudal Japan during the Golden Age of Ninjutsu, when the ninja carried his short sword, *shuriken* and other multipurpose weapons. Or maybe your mind will develop an updated version of the "secret warrior," with a silenced mini-submachine gun and an array of electronic gadgetry one step ahead of James Bond but just this side of *Star Wars*. Your ninja's assignments will probably require the special skills that only he and a few like him have been able to perfect as a result of years of secret, mysterious, superhuman training and activity.

Step from the shadows Steve Hayes, a trim six-foot, 165-pound, quiet, mild-mannered, polite, handsome man and all those images you've built up in your mind about sinister assassins fly out the window. But Hayes is a ninja . . . the one with the best credentials living in the United States. He is a teacher, practitioner and student of Togakure Ryu, the thirty-fourth-generation system of ninjutsu, directed by Dr. Masaaki Hatsumi in Noda City, Japan.

"At one time there were several schools within the ninja art," he explained to Chris McLoughlin, who has interviewed Hayes on many occasions, "but our style is the only one with a traceable history now surviving. Of course, there are others who practice in their backyards and on the sly, but we don't know much about them. Our style is the only one in existence that is acknowledged by the Japanese government."

Hayes, now living in Ohio where he is translating into English works of Dr. Hatsumi and writing his own book on ninjutsu, isn't at all pleased with the image most people have of the ninja.

"Actually," Hayes patiently explained, "most of those men who hired out as assassins and spies weren't really ninja at all. They were merely thugs and gangsters who had some experience with the martial arts, and they wore black clothing."

Though he doesn't approve, Hayes does understand why these misconceptions about the ninja exist. In Japan, for example, where you would expect a more accurate understanding of the art, ninja are familiar to all as the spooky, slippery, black-clad bad guys that appear in children's novels, cartoon strips and on TV serials.

"When one mentions 'ninja' to a Japanese," Hayes says, "he is almost sure to get a universally performed response. The Japanese will smile, grip the middle and index fingers of his left hand in his right fist, and position his hands vertically in front of his chest while uttering *'Daron, daron!'* This is an inaccurate imitation of the ninja's *kuji-in* hand positioning and a traditional sort of magic word. All Japanese are apparently taught this stock reaction and are expected to display it when hearing the word 'ninja.' This is similar to the manner in which Americans are taught to yell 'Hi-yo Silver!' whenever they hear the William Tell Overture."

Though the fiction in Japan has emphasized the sinister—the warrior who was the master of terrible weapons and elaborate tricks—Hayes found it interesting while he was there to note that their immediate reaction had to do more with the psychic aspects of the art than with the fighting techniques.

"To most Japanese," Hayes explained, "the ninja were traditionally masters of other-worldly powers, such as mind reading, disappearing at will and controlling the destinies of others, even though many Japanese feel that these effects were accomplished through a deception of the senses.

"The Western concept, on the other hand, tends to picture the ninja as a sort of feudal commando. The ninja was a master of dirty fighting, sneaking around and murdering people in their sleep. Ninjutsu is referred to as a martial art along with karate and judo, and seems to be regarded as a series of physical skills to destroy an enemy. To become a ninja, therefore, one merely trains the bones and muscles to perform a variety of fighting techniques."

As far as Hayes is concerned, the true, historical ninja lies somewhere between the "Japanese Mystic of the Mountains" and the Western "Killer for Hire." He is a man capable of destruction, but his major concern is with total enlightenment. By divorcing themselves from the original tenets of ninjutsu, by perfecting their physical skills and ignoring the philosophy upon which ninjutsu was based, Hayes feels that these men surrendered the right to call themselves ninja.

By combining both aspects of ninjutsu in their training, the physical and the philosophical, the instructors of the Togakure Ryu system are trying to remove the stigma attached to the ninja today and build an image that more closely resembles the ascetics who first developed the art.

For a number of years, prior to developing an interest in ninjutsu, Hayes taught a traditional style of Korean karate. He was at odds with many of the classical techniques that he showed his students and found himself constantly explaining that this concept was wrong or that technique was no longer valid because times had changed, and people didn't fight like that anymore.

About the same time these realizations came to light for him, he read a series of articles and some books on the mysterious art of ninjutsu. It appealed to him on a purely physical level. It seemed to offer techniques that were far more practical than those of the system he taught.

"All during the time that I was teaching classical karate," he says, "I thought to myself that there ought to be more to it than just this. I wasn't necessarily looking for anything in particular, and certainly nothing mysterious or religious, but there was no light at the end of the tunnel, and I was growing bored and frustrated with what I was doing."

After chasing down the source of the material he had read, Hayes applied for training with Tsunehisa Tanemura and Dr. Masaaki Hatsumi in Noda-Shi, Japan. When he didn't receive a reply, he turned his school in Atlanta, Georgia, over to his students and headed off to Japan to track down Dr. Hatsumi.

Hayes recalls with a smile the events leading up to his first meeting with Hatsumi. "I'd written to him several months before I left for Japan. Though he didn't reply, I knew he was there. So off I went. The trip was exhausting, but I finally reached my destination, Noda City, secured a room and arranged to meet with Dr. Hatsumi.

"Later that evening, a car pulled up in front of the hotel, and out he stepped, dressed casually in jeans and a sport shirt. I didn't know what I was expecting, but this certainly wasn't it." After some conversation with Dr. Hatsumi and his associate, Hayes asked if they had received his letter. "Yes," Dr. Hatsumi told him, "but we knew you'd be coming anyway, so there was no need to answer it."

"When I heard that answer," Hayes recalled, "I thought to myself, 'you just might be in the right place after all.' "

Hayes was honored to be the first American to be accepted as a *Uchi-Deshi* ("personal student in the home of the grandmaster") in the history of Togakure Ryu ninjutsu. "After my initial training sessions in the moonlit rice fields of rural Saitama

Prefecture," Steve says, "my feelings of being honored changed to an awareness that I had at last found the 'ultimate' fighting art for me. Here was a system of totally practical fighting techniques, not at all diluted for sport or the sake of the art, kept alive by a small group of serious, enlightened individuals."

One of the things that impressed Hayes most was the fact that on a fighting level, the techniques of the Togakure Ryu system are constantly revised and updated, thus making it a living art, rather than one that has stifled itself with techniques that are impractical for modern-day use.

Hayes remained in Japan for over a year, his enthusiasm for the art never once waning. And when he was ready to return home to Atlanta, Dr. Hatsumi awarded him a teacher's certificate. To this date, it is the only one in the United States and one of the few in the entire world.

"I was in an awkward position when I got back to Atlanta," he says seriously. "Now I had an art that I wasn't ashamed of and that I didn't have to apologize for while teaching it, but there were very few folks who'd ever heard of ninjutsu. Karate was the popular and 'in' thing to learn, but I was determined not to be discouraged."

Working toward the goal of returning to Japan to resume his studies with Dr. Hatsumi, Hayes began teaching everything he had learned to his two senior students, Larry Beaver and Bud Malmstrom. He also arranged for one of Hatsumi's leading instructors (the one who had been by Steve's side through most of his training), Tsunehisa Tanemura, to come over for a visit and run some special classes. That was in 1975; and in 1977, Hayes once again packed his bags and headed for Japan, remaining until 1980.

On his return to Japan, Hayes began establishing roots. Living in a small apartment outside Tokyo, he began teaching his art at a small club. A bilingual American living in Japan has no shortage of opportunities, and Steve was able to pick and choose his income-producing activities. During his stay there he appeared on the Japanese version of the Johnny Carson show, where he began to bring the true art of ninjutsu out of the shadows for the people whose own heritage it was. In addition to those activities, Hayes played the part of a cowboy in a Xerox company motivation film entitled "The Thirty-Second Sniper."

When it was discovered that there was an American living in Japan who knew ninjutsu and could maintain a sense of presence in front of a camera, Hayes was immediately drafted for a part in the television feature, *Shōgun*. He also was consulted by the directors on the martial arts and, of course, the ninja scenes. But still, with all these activities, Steve remained true to his purpose for being there, and everything else took second place to Dr. Hatsumi and his classes.

The severe training in austere surroundings tested the dedication of Hayes as well as the other students. "Students begin their training with extremely difficult physical exercises and drills," Hayes recalls. "Breakfalls for throws are practiced on bare wooden floors. Proper 'feel' of the fundamental actions of evasion and blocking is stressed as the student begins to practice the basics of the unarmed combat system. Those who try to leave the physical training too soon and begin asking questions about 'spirit' are admonished to quit thinking and train harder.

"Once he attains black belt rank and is formally accepted into the familylike organization, the student continues his physical training along with the addition of a few mental exercises."

Dr. Hatsumi teaches his advanced students exercises that will help them relax and make full use of their body's energy. Some of these exercises cover the mental processes of the attacker and defender during a conflict. They also learn to develop mental flexibility and to be able to adapt to surprises during a fight.

At the Togakure Ryu, only those who have advanced to the rank of *Shihan* ("master teacher") are given direct instruction in the "spiritual" or Third Level techniques. "Physical demonstrations of these extraordinary methods are given for the lower-ranked students," explains Hayes, "but no comments are ever made as to how the skills are developed. When asked about the higher levels of training, the Shihan simply recommends that the student keep working at his own level, and he will automatically attain what he desires."

It was during his second session in Japan that Steve's personal philosophies on ninjutsu began to emerge. "For me this is a personal art for winning, for getting the things I need and want and still have the world better for it," he says. "Ninjutsu is there for us to use; we're not there for the art. It's not practiced for the preservation of the art itself, but so that I and others can have a better life from having used it. It helps me to understand myself and the people I deal with, and it develops an attitude of enlightenment which makes everything better for me."

Hayes now teaches a small class in Ohio, keeps in touch with his original school in Atlanta, and presents seminars on ninjutsu throughout the country. While it is his responsibility, as it is the responsibility of each new headmaster, to update the training methods of the system so that Togakure Ryu Ninjutsu will never become antiquated, the history and traditions are still preserved. Today, as taught by Dr. Hatsumi and Hayes, there are eight training steps for Togakure Ryu: unarmed fighting, leaping methods, wooden staff fighting, blade fighting and throwing, chain and sword weapons, the use of natural elements for escape, the art of disguise and military strategy. Further, within these eight training steps, there are three major levels of knowledge. The first is physical and parallels the methods used by the *genin* of old. The techniques of body agility and proficiency in fighting are taught from a practical standpoint rather than as a system of elaborate skills; a few fundamentals are perfected to cover a multitude of situations.

The second level is mental and corresponds to the *chunin* in the ninja hierarchy. It is here that psychological lessons and strategy are applied to physical techniques. Here the ninja becomes aware of the five "feelings" (*go jo*) in others. He learns to deal with the vain, cowardly, hot-tempered, lazy and soft-hearted adversaries. In addition, the ninja learns to deal with the five basic "desires" (*go yoku*) in others: hunger, sex, pride, pleasure and greed. Beyond knowing that these concepts exist, the ninja must be adept at sizing up others and knowing which of these principles to use against them.

Also within this second level, the ninja must be

prepared and be able to teach his skill to others. Military strategy and the concepts of how best to use combat skills are stressed.

To "feel" is an important part of the second level. One student once asked Dr. Hatsumi, "What if I were perched sniperlike on top of a building with a strong scope and rifle aimed at the door you were about to exit? What defense could you possibly use?" Dr. Hatsumi's answer was: "I must be able to sense the danger and not go out the door."

The spiritual level comes third and corresponds closely to the *jonin* level. It is characterized by a strengthening and understanding of the spirit through years of self-examination. At this stage, the warrior evolves to the philosopher. Here the ninja strives through nine specific steps for enlightenment, from the base, physical aspects to spiritual perfection (*Kuji Kiri*). Each of these nine steps is represented by a position of the hands with fingers entwined (*mudra*), a vocalized word of concentration (*mantra*), and a specific goal of accomplishment.

So the centuries-old system of fighting techniques, information gathering and psychological controls is constantly being updated and taught with an eye to the traditional ties of the past, but in terms of modern practicality. In contrast to the rigid and formalized classical Oriental karate classes that emphasize a solid stand-your-ground-powerfully, do-or-die attitude, the ninja classes stress a fluidity, deceptive movement and most important, an organized thought process behind their fighting techniques. As for the currently popular jumping, turning, spinning, flashing moves go, Hayes doesn't teach any because, for the ninja, they just wouldn't be of any practical use. For empty-hand fighting success, Hayes stresses low area kicks, strikes to vital areas and joints, some throws which he complements with locks and holds.

Hayes is the first to admit that he gets a lot of less-than-serious inquiries. "We get our share of the crazies who want to join us; people who think we are some mystic cult or that we're teaching the 'death touch' and so forth." (One person who contacted Hayes mentioned in his letter that he had trained a band of "gorillas.") Steve has been contacted by self-styled ninja who have offered to help provide assistance on any of his nocturnal assignments, but Hayes's reply to these is, "Well, to my knowledge, none of my students hire out as hit men on the side. We are pursuing our training as a means of awareness and self-development."

Hayes is proud of his art and the nonstructured growth that it maintains to flourish. As new developments appear on the horizon, they are swiftly incorporated into the Togakure Ryu system. Computers, sophisticated firearms, electronic gadgetry and other modern wizardry are just as much a part of the ninja's arsenal as are swords, *shuriken*, blowguns and chains. It is left up to the individual to pick and choose what he will utilize to help him reach his particular goals. In Hayes's words, "The modern ninjutsu system is not merely a collection of specifics, but a compendium from which the ninja draws so that he is able to fight, to think and to accomplish."

Recently, Dr. Hatsumi bestowed a promotion upon Hayes, and with it a task. Hayes is now the man in charge of establishing and promoting the Togakure Ryu system of ninjutsu in the United

States, and Hatsumi has given blanket approval
and backing for any action taken in that direction.
In terms of organization, the road is clear and
open to whatever Hayes feels is the most appropriate action to get the job done. In a sense, Hayes
has become the "PR" man of the ninja, and one
step he has taken in that direction is the regular
publishing of a newsletter, The Shadows of Iga,
(for information on that, one can contact Larry
Beaver, Beaver Products, P.O. Box 1580, Anna
Maria, Florida 33501), which is currently being
distributed from Japan.

In Ohio, Hayes tries to follow the same disciplines of mental and physical development that
were mandatory while he studied with Dr. Hatsumi in Japan. Though his surroundings don't
provide the same mystique he found in the Orient,
he has learned to adjust and improvise, like the
true ninja he is, and come up with a program of
training that produces comparable results.

He rises early each morning and has a spartan
breakfast of Japanese soup. He then walks and
runs for approximately an hour, keeping his mind
clear and open to the stimulation provided by his
environment. This hour could be described as a
period of moving meditation.

The fields of Ohio aren't at all like the magical
hills of Japan that seem to have been designed
for ninja training, but Hayes has found a spot
near his home that does provide the terrain and
seclusion necessary for his workouts.

"It's a gravel pit with water . . . more like a
pool," he says. "I go there alone or with my wife
or one of my students after my run and practice
with one of my weapons."

Each day, he chooses a different weapon to

work with. One day it will be the stick or staff. The next day he might devote the major portion of his morning to knife throwing. Hayes does not use a formal throwing knife. He prefers the U.S. Marine utility knife, which is inexpensive, rugged and deadly when handled correctly. And it can be handled correctly and become an effective throwing weapon only through constant, intense practice. He goes over the same moves hundreds of times each two-hour session, checking his footwork and timing, until they become second nature to him and the weapon becomes an extension of his body.

While at the gravel pit, Hayes will go through an hour of exercises (*junan taiso*), which could be called the ninja yoga. He stretches and bends and does some calisthenics. Following that, particularly if there is someone along to work with, he will practice breakfalls, jumps and footwork, those nonviolent techniques that make the ninja such an elusive, difficult-to-pin-down opponent.

Hayes breaks his training for a light lunch. Seventy percent of his diet is made up of Japanese foods—unpolished rice, Japanese soups, grains and salads. The other thirty percent is standard American fare, except that he avoids potatoes, which he doesn't like. But there is no limit to what he and other ninja will eat. Dr. Hatsumi, for example, prefers the difficult-to-get (especially in Japan) unpolished rice and vegetables, but he will eat whatever is placed before him if dining out with friends. One more example of ninja versatility.

In the afternoon, Hayes will divide his time between writing and training. He doesn't have a rigid schedule. He doesn't designate any particular time for either activity. He likes to be spontaneous, which is definitely a result of his training as a ninja. If one day writing has the greater appeal, he'll spend most of the afternoon at his desk. If he feels he needs more physical than mental activity that day, he'll put most of his hours in at the gravel pit.

"If I write all day," Hayes explains, "I feel uncomfortable. My body rebels. I become bored. But I also have found that during those times when I taught only physical techniques, my life was equally as boring. I need the balance between physical activity and creativeness.

"Dr. Hatsumi feels the same way. He enjoys painting to fulfill his creative needs, but he could never do it as a full-time activity. Most of the master teachers in Japan have other interests, hobbies if you wish, to balance their lives. One I know enjoys singing and others, like Dr. Hatsumi, enjoy working with the brush."

But sometime during the afternoon, Hayes will return to the gravel pit to continue polishing his ninja techniques as well as teaching those techniques to one or more of his students.

The pit is a very suitable setting for ninja training. There are walls that can be scaled, a pool that can be used for water techniques and brush that can be used for concealment exercises.

"I will send one or more of my people into the brush," he says, "and they are confined to a limited area to conceal themselves. I then go in and try to flush them out."

There may also be some additional weapons training, using the traditional ninja implements, like the *shuriken,* as well as modern weapons.

"During the training periods," said Hayes, "I

don't go out in a sixteenth-century ninja suit. I wear jeans and a denim jacket or a sweatsuit and running shoes. If anybody does see me, I don't want to appear too weird or shocking."

Because Hayes doesn't have a formal school, his evening classes in unarmed training, which begin after dinner and last until 9:30 P.M., are held in the gym of a local country club. It is strictly a session in classical or revised ninja techniques; nothing is taken from other styles of Oriental unarmed combat like karate, jujutsu or kung fu.

"I don't believe in style. It's not a word I use," Hayes explains. "Whatever comes up in a combat situation can be handled by techniques in ninjutsu. What we teach is not an art form but a way to fight. In fact, a good street fighter will have all the basic abilities to become a good ninja."

He will become a good ninja if his fighting form is given polish by an instructor like Hayes.

At the gym, Hayes emphasizes the low, wide fighting stance used by the ninja for combat with or without weapons. It is a solid stance which makes the ninja posture stable and difficult to upset. His center of gravity is set low enough for him to become as difficult to move as a boulder. From this stance, the ninja can attack with the low techniques he prefers. Hayes discourages the high, fast, swinging kicks that are especially popular with Korean stylists. Having studied and taught Korean karate before turning to ninjutsu, his experience has proved to him that they aren't practical. Direct attack is what he believes in, and what he teaches.

After his evening classes, Hayes returns home to unwind. He lets his mind relax with music, the closest he comes to pure meditation. He thinks about his writing or other projects he has planned.

"I guess you could call it a form of meditation," he says, "though I don't consider it that. I let my mind relax whenever I think it is appropriate, not only before going to sleep. I can even do it when I'm engaged in physical activities, like when I'm throwing my knife. I separate my thoughts from what my body is doing."

After a half hour or an hour of relaxation, Hayes is ready for sleep. It's the end of a day in the life of a ninja.

Not long ago, Hayes stated that his art had remained in the shadows for hundreds of years and that there was no sign that it might emerge in modern times. But things do change, thanks to present-day communications and the American penchant for mystery laced with fantasy and excitement, and with them so do the prospects that ninjutsu will come into its own in the public eye. Certainly, Steve Hayes is here to see that the phantom of yesterday becomes a reality of tomorrow.

Ninja
Tales

DEATH BY SWORD

Jiro sat by the edge of the road, his body shaking with pain and fever. The last rays of the sun shimmered on the Mimito river. The beauty of the sunset and the serene majesty of the palace of Kyoto in the distance was the wrong setting for what he had just experienced and witnessed. There should be thunder, lightning and winds to bring unity to this cruel scene.

The wails of the unseen dying stabbed at him. The sounds spurred his memory, and he brought his trembling hand up along his sweat-stained cheek until it contacted the sticky ooze that had once been his eye. He quickly pulled his hand away as the image of his mutilation began to build in his mind. For long moments, he clawed the air around his face, drawn to the gaping hole, but unable to touch it. Suddenly, in panic, he began to crawl toward the river, his own cries now joining the chorus of the dying.

Once on the shore, he plunged his head into the

cool water . . . withdrawing it and plunging it in again . . . until the searing pain that tore through his head was numbed. The water lessened his panic. His breathing slowed. His mind began to clear.

"I must rest," he told himself as he tore a piece of cloth from the sleeve of his kimono, soaked it in the water and placed it over the cavity where his eye had been.

"I am a ninja. I must clear my mind of all thoughts of pain and fear. I must recapture and control my inner spirit. I must calm my mind and heal my body. . . . I must calm my mind and heal my body. . . . I must calm my mind and heal my body. . . ."

He lay back on the soft grass, his mind clear, and let his weariness take control of his body.

The day had begun joyfully for Jiro. He had been awakened by the laughter of Toyotoro, his small son, and the scent of tea being prepared by his wife, Shakin. He had propped himself on one elbow on the torn *tatami* that served as his bed and watched Shakin as she moved about the tiny hut preparing for the new day. She was short with full figure and a strong square face, with almost masculine features. Most people would consider her plain, even homely, but to Jiro she was a prize . . . a woman of humor, inner beauty and strength who was completely devoted to her family. Jiro was well satisfied and often thanked the Spirits for making him wise enough to choose her for his wife.

"You are finally awake," Shakin said as she poured his tea. "The sun has been our guest for over an hour, and we have already had visitors."

Jiro sipped the tea and watched Shakin, her ample figure straining at the *uchigi* she wore.

"Who comes visiting at so early an hour?"

"It was Inenbo with a warning," Shakin said. "The warriors of Takatoki, led by many samurai, arrive today from the Kanto Plain. They have looted many villages along their march, so Inenbo has said, and they have raped and killed with great savagery. He says we must hide, or at least remain indoors. I laughed at him. He is plagued by spirits and imagines great harm will come to us. I told him I would send you to him the moment you awoke. But I do not believe there is need for much haste."

Naïve woman, Jiro thought, sobered by what she had said. So loving she could not imagine cruelty. Inenbo, leader of the ninja clan, was not a teller of tales. If he saw fit to bring a warning, then they were in danger.

Why were the Fujiwara so weak, Jiro asked himself as he quickly dressed. They were the ruling family, but it was the warrior cliques who really ruled the empire. Taira Kiyomori and his samurai control the emperor and his court in Kyoto, and now Takatoki and his warriors came to challenge them. Will there never be peace?

Jiro tied his *hakama* over his kimono, pushed his short sword into his *obi* and hurried to see Inenbo. He judged by the deserted road that all in the village had received the warning. Inenbo was wise and would know what to do. He had served as a spy, courier and assassin for the Taira. He had been to court. He was learned. He would find a solution.

"You look for a solution, Jiro, but there is none," Inenbo said, his manner calm, almost serene. Only his eyes revealed the intensity within. "If the whole clan leaves the village, Takatoki's warriors will quickly notice and track us down. Many are on horseback, and they are well armed. We will be no match for them.

"But"—he now sat up straight, revealing his broad shoulders and strong neck—"if we choose some of the woman, most of the children and a few strong men to go with them and protect them, and send them to the hills, no one will know they are missing. No one will look for them. The village will appear occupied as it has always been. And then if the worst does occur, if we do suffer the same fate as the other villages, at least some of the clan will be saved."

"Saved? Saved for how long?" Jiro asked bitterly.

"We can plan only for today," Inenbo said quietly, understanding the anguish of the young, untested ninja. "We can only hope for tomorrow. And now, we must work quickly. We must choose who will go and who will stay."

The plan was brutally simple. If there were four or less members of a family, only one would be allowed to leave. If there were five, two would be permitted to go. Six or seven, three; eight, four; nine or ten, five. There were no families in the clan with more than ten members. Inenbo had decided. He was the leader, and backed by Jiro, no one would openly object to his plan.

The next two hours were as busy as they were sad. For Jiro and Shakin, the decision was heartbreakingly simple. They would send their son to safety. For the larger families, the decisions were, if possible, even more painful. Mothers had to choose between children; husbands had to choose between wives and parents. There were tears and entreaties, but when the two hours had elapsed, the oxcarts were loaded, and those chosen to be saved were ready to leave.

"You must not look back, and you must not return until you receive word that all is safe," Inenbo told those who were leaving. "We are a peaceful people, but we are strong. We cannot battle armies, but we will survive if we persevere and use well our great gift of intelligence."

Jiro wanted to embrace Toyotoro as Shakin had, but it might appear to be a display of weakness not appropriate now. The boy was young. To him this was an adventure, not a disaster. If they were not to meet again, he must grow to manhood remembering his father as strong and fearless, a man devoid of emotion, a man who was a leader as *he* would someday be a leader.

The caravan had barely left the village when Inenbo called Jiro aside.

"We must not fight unless forced to. We have not the strength or the numbers to compete with these samurai in open warfare. We must use intelligence and guile if we are to survive."

The soldiers of Takatoki arrived at sunset. Many were on foot, peasant slaves of the warlord. They were led by a hundred samurai on horseback, in armor of strips of bright metal held together by colored cloth. Their leader, astride a huge chestnut horse, wore a deep green hunting garment of fine cloth under his armor. The scabbard of his long sword, which he wore across his back, was lacquered a deep brown and encrusted with gold, silver and precious stones. He dismounted and fully revealed a hiramon saddle, one that was lacquered and also decorated with gold, silver and gems.

Though he had short legs, his torso was massive, and it was obvious that he was extremely strong. He was close to forty, but his face was youthful, marred only by a blood-red scar that ran from the corner of his right eye to his chin. His head was uncovered, revealing jet black hair pulled back to form the traditional knot.

He barked orders in a deep commanding voice to his men to dismount and stand ready. His personal slave rushed to his side to hand him his long bow and three colored and white eagle-tailed arrows. The samurai leader handed his slave the reins of his horse and walked alone down the road toward the center of the village. There were no sounds or signs of life. The houses built on either side of the road were hushed and still behind the wooden shutters and bulrush blinds.

"Where is your leader?" he called when he arrived at the center of the village. But no one answered.

"Where is the coward you call your leader? Where is the man called Inenbo, the traitor who has served the Taira against my master, Takatoki? Let him come before me like a man before we set torch to this village of vermin and drive him out."

The warriors behind him shuffled in anticipation. They knew their leader. They would soon have food and drink, women and sport.

The door of Inenbo's house opened slowly and the ninja leader, followed by Jiro, walked to the center of the street, their eyes never leaving the face of the armored samurai.

"How can I serve you?" Inenbo addressed the samurai. His voice was calm; only the white spittle that formed in the corners of his mouth revealed the fear he felt.

The samurai placed an arrow in his bow. "You will bring food and drink for my men, and you will order your women to service them. But first you will crawl to me on your hands and knees like the dog that you are to beg for your life."

Jiro's hand flew to the handle of his sword, but he was stopped by Inenbo who whispered, "Let us not rush to our death. It will come soon enough."

Inenbo walked slowly toward the samurai. "Food and drink I can give you, but I cannot provide your other demands. I alone have enraged your lord. Let me then stand the test of your might. Meet me alone in combat and let my people go in peace. None of them have harmed you or your lord."

The samurai was enraged and hissed his reply. "Ninja have been the thorn in our side for many years. You have attacked our caravans and killed our merchants and warriors. You have been the agents of evil spirits and have killed in darkness without thought of honor. And now you seek an honorable death.

"But I will not grant you the privilege of an honorable end," the samurai said calmly and quietly. He turned his back on Inenbo and walked toward his men. "You and your people will die like the dogs that you are."

If he signaled his men, it was imperceptible. Suddenly, there was an eruption of movement and noise among the warriors. The sound of swords being drawn from scabbards and cries of battle filled the air. Rearing horses raised clouds of dust, birds fled from the eaves of houses, loudly squawking their displeasure at being disturbed.

Jiro and Inenbo stood helplessly by as hordes of soldiers rushed down both side of the street and invaded the shuttered homes. Inenbo was quickly surrounded by six sturdy samurai who advanced menacingly toward him with their swords drawn and raised over their heads. Jiro was prevented from helping Inenbo by three samurai who blocked his way. He watched helplessly as Inenbo drew his short sword and reached into his sash to bring forth a weighted chain, the deadly *manriki gusari,* which he then slowly whirled about his head as the circle of samurai closed about him.

As the first samurai lunged, Inenbo whipped the chain around his sword-wielding arm, pulled him forward and off balance, and drove his sword into his chest. Turning quickly to face two attacking together, he ducked under the slashing sword of one and drove his blade up under the chin into the brain. Rolling quickly toward the second samurai, he buried his sword in the man's groin.

Jiro backed slowly away from the three men stalking him as he watched the amazing performance of Inenbo. His own sword was still undrawn. As he reached to draw it, he felt a chill: he had heard the frightened cries of Shakin. Forgetting the danger in front of him, he turned to see Shakin being dragged by her hair from his house by two peasant warriors. Her face was twisted by fear as her bulging eyes pleaded with him for help.

Ignoring the samurai behind him, he rushed toward his wife, his sword whirling about his head. His blade found the soft part of the neck of the first warrior and almost severed his head. As he withdrew the sword, the dying man's blood surged from the wound, staining the cowering

Shakin. He then turned on the second peasant who, so surprised by the attack, reacted by covering his face with his hands. Jiro lunged at his unprotected chest and drove his sword straight through his heart.

Before he could touch his sobbing wife to comfort her, he was seized from behind by two other samurai and pinned to the wall of his hut. Yet another, legs astride the still prone Shakin, placed the point of his sword against Jiro's chest.

"You think your woman is too good for the warriors of Takatoki?" he snarled. "Let us find out just how good she is."

As Jiro struggled helplessly, the samurai bent over Shakin and tore open her outer garment. Her body quivered uncontrollably as he ripped her undergarment, the *uchigi* Jiro had admired a few hours earlier, with the tip of his sharp sword until the treasures of her body were fully revealed. Jiro screamed in agony as the samurai lowered himself on top of the almost lifeless body and raped her.

"She is not worthy of my energy," the samurai said as he rose and straightened his clothes. "See how lifeless she is," he said to Jiro. And as the stunned ninja looked on, the samurai placed the tip of his sword between her legs and tore open her flesh up to her breasts.

The cries of Jiro and the dying Shakin joined those of the other villagers who had been herded into the street to be raped and slaughtered. Jiro groaned as he looked past his dying wife and saw the tortures being committed. He watched with horror as a samurai ran by with the still-living third son of Inenbo impaled on his swinging sword.

And then he saw Inenbo, pinned to the wall of

his hut by a dozen arrows, the leader of the samurai standing before him and mocking him as he slowly died.

Jiro turned his head and closed his eyes. He felt the sickness in his stomach rise to his mouth; sour vomit trickled from his lips.

"You find the view distressing," he heard the samurai who had killed Shakin say to him, his voice echoing as if coming from a tunnel. "Let me help you then."

He felt strong hands pull his head straight, and he opened his eyes just in time to see the point of the sword enter to pluck his eye from its socket.

The hands holding him let him slip to the ground. Dark blood dripped and stained the sand, and just before he fainted he heard the samurai say, "We leave you now. We leave you to your memories and a slow, lingering death."

The cry of scavenging crows woke Jiro to the stench of decomposing bodies. The sun burned his face and aggravated his wound. His one eye focused slowly as he rose on weak, shaking legs, his arms searching for support where there was none. He looked down at his *hakama,* stained with the pungent smell of his own blood, and he once again felt nausea rise.

He began to stagger toward the village, falling frequently. The death stench grew stronger the closer he came to his hut. He passed bloated bodies oozing water and covered with blue flies, and he vomited when he came upon a pack of dogs chewing on the body of a child.

He began to tremble as he approached the spot where Shakin had died. A wild hope seized him. Perhaps it hadn't really happened. He might have imagined Shakin's torture. She would now be in his hut preparing his tea, and they would once again be happy and live peacefully.

But his dream was shattered as he stepped onto the road that ran through the village. Shakin lay where she had been killed. A white, fly-covered scum covered her gaping stomach. The sockets of her eyes were empty. Her face was horribly distorted, her mouth open wide, as if she was about to scream.

It was Jiro who screamed, scattering the crows and sending the dogs howling with fright. He pulled at his hair and sobbed as he fled, staggering, toward the hills.

Three months had passed when the leader of the forces of Takatoki received the message at the Imperial Palace in Kyoto. It was a challenge to a duel of honor from one Jiro, who called himself the leader of the ninja.

"I know no Jiro," the samurai addressed his lieutenants, "but if he is truly the leader of the ninja clan, he must be dealt with.

"He presents conditions. He will fight me in fair open combat with the long sword, and if I die by his sword, he wants me to pledge as a samurai that I will no longer wage war on his people. If I live, all members of the clan who are still alive will surrender themselves to me to be dealt with as I wish."

The samurai thought for a long moment. If I refuse, he thought, the ninja will brand me a coward, and I will lose face. If I accept, I will surely win, and I will rid the land of this ninja clan once and for all. I dare not refuse. "Send him word that I agree," he said to the messenger.

The site chosen by Jiro for the duel was the dusty road that ran through the village, now deserted and in disrepair, mute testimony to the horror that had occurred. When the samurai arrived, accompanied by twenty of his most trusted warriors, Jiro was waiting for him in the center of the road, a black patch covering his healing wound. He was haggard and worn, feverish.

"Is this the great warrior who challenges me?" the samurai said as he approached Jiro on foot.

Jiro stood silently, his legs spread wide, his unsheathed sword held in both hands before him. He glared at the samurai with his one eye and when he spoke, after many long moments, his voice was barely a whisper.

"You have agreed to the conditions. If you die by my sword, you have sworn on your honor as a samurai that your warriors will no longer harm my people, and they will be allowed to live peacefully in this village once again."

The samurai smiled at the lean, almost skeletal figure before him. "I have made that pledge, and the warriors who are with me here bear witness to it. But if I do not die by your sword, all of your clan who still live will surrender themselves to me. That is understood?"

Jiro nodded.

The samurai then lowered himself cross-legged to the ground, removed his sword, still in its scabbard, from his *obi,* and placed it on the sand before him. He closed his eyes and payed homage to the spirit of the sword. Jiro did not move. He stood and watched the ceremony calmly, disinterested, as if he was not a part of the action that was about to take place.

The samurai rose, placed his sword in his *obi,*

then ceremoniously unsheathed it. The other samurai formed a wide circle around the two warriors.

The samurai leader circled Jiro defiantly, his long sword clutched in one hand. Jiro stood his ground, turning slowly so that he always faced his opponent. Suddenly the samurai lashed out. Jiro blocked the blow, but the force almost tore the sword from his hands. Jiro lunged awkwardly, the attack so slow the samurai did not need to parry it. He stepped aside nimbly and smiled. His adversary was a brave man, but not a trained swordsman. He was obviously weak and unsure of himself. This would be an easy victory.

The sound of the clashing of swords echoed through the hills. The samurai toyed with Jiro, who felt his arms becoming heavy and weak. He lunged and slashed and then allowed the ninja to recover to show his disdain for Jiro's ability.

When Jiro was close to collapse, the smile left the samurai's face. "I've played with you long enough. Now you must die."

His sword whistled through the air and sunk into the neck of the defenseless Jiro, slicing him almost to his chest. Jiro uttered not a sound. Blood filled his mouth as he sunk to the ground and fell forward on his face.

He was dead.

The samurai knelt beside Jiro and cleaned his sword on his opponent's *hakama*. A brave but foolish warrior, the samurai thought. As he began to rise, he noticed Jiro's sword, still clutched in the ninja's hand. It was a simple weapon, not one of quality. It was completely devoid of ornament except for one beautiful jewel at the top of the handle.

The samurai took the sword from Jiro's hand

and examined the jewel. It was a perfect, brilliant stone carved with great care and craftsmanship. It would become a fine addition to the samurai's collection.

The samurai was trying to pry it loose when he heard the sound of the spring and felt the sharp needle enter his finger. The poison began to act immediately. The samurai stared at his hand with disbelief. As he weakened, a smile formed on his lips. Calling his men to his side, he gave his final order.

"I pledged the safety of this ninja clan if Jiro could defeat me with his sword. Now you will honor my pledge. Jiro has truly killed me with his sword."

CHANGE OF HEART

The figure in black eased himself silently over the stone wall that surrounded the tranquil garden and dropped noiselessly to the ground. He pressed his back against the shadowed wall and stood motionless as he waited for his eyes to become accustomed to the dark. He looked to the sky and thanked the Gods for sending black clouds to cover the moon.

While his eyes were unable to help him, he strained his ears for sounds of danger and sniffed the air for human odors. Satisfied he had not been seen or heard by the guards, he moved carefully along the wall, his padded sandals muffling the sounds of his footsteps. He clutched the short sword strapped to his back with one hand to prevent its striking the jutting stones.

As his eyes slowly became accustomed to the blackness, he could see the outline of the wood and clay tile palace of the warlord Nakamura. He had entered the garden at the closest point to the house,

but he was still a great distance from Lord Nakamura's bedchamber.

Reaching the house would not be easy. Though
it was hidden in the darkness, he knew there was
a large pond, dotted with tiny islands, that would
have to be crossed. The narrow bridge would be
guarded and would present a formidable obstacle.
And though there were trees along the route he
would take that could provide cover, he would be
in the open for most of the distance and could
be seen if the moon was to break from the clouds.

He listened to the sounds of the crickets and
breathed deep the sweet smell of blossoming chrysanthemums as he drew the long, thin wire from
the sash around his waist. He would kill tonight.
He would kill more than once in this setting that
seemed more appropriate for the contemplation of
beauty and life.

He wrapped the ends of the wire around each
of his gloved hands, crouched low and began moving toward the palace.

Lord Nakamura slid back the wall panel of his
bedchamber and looked out into the dark garden.
He, too, heard the crickets and breathed the same
strong perfume of chrysanthemums, but he was
too engrossed with his thoughts to be affected by
the pleasing sound and scent.

He wore a simple white kimono that hung
loosely on his gaunt frame. His hair, dark as the
night, was untied and reached past his shoulders.
His eyes were cold, his lips thin and cruel. His
face was the mirror of his many years as warlord.
There was no sign of pity or compassion reflected
in it.

"He's out there, isn't he?" he said as if thinking

aloud. "Perhaps he's even watching me this very moment."

His most trusted samurai moved toward his master, staying close to the wall so as not to be seen by anyone in the garden.

"It is the time we arranged," he whispered. "He has been paid well. I am sure he is there."

Nakamura closed the panel and walked back into the room.

"There is no possibility the guards know he is coming? He must not be stopped before reaching this room."

"Only you and I know of the arrangement," the samurai assured him. "The guards outside your room have been told you have had a vision of death and that they must be doubly alert. I will shortly call them into your room and order them to remain with me by your side through the night. I will also order one of them to occupy your bed. We will leave nothing to chance. As for the guards in the garden, they have been told nothing."

Nakamura nodded his understanding as he sat on the small dressing stool by his bed.

"You have served me well," he said without looking up. "Now tell me: who is this ninja you have hired to kill me?"

"His name is Tahishi," the samurai said. "He is from Iga and has performed many remarkable feats. It is he who penetrated the Kogoshu of the Imperial Palace and brought back word of the plans of the Regent Nobunaga by listening unseen at the meeting he held with his warlords.

"He has killed many times and has served many warlords. He has even been employed by the great Nobunaga himself."

"Then you have chosen the right man," Nakamura said. "It is good that Nobunaga will recognize him when we display his body and the samurai he has killed in his attempt to assassinate me. Nobunaga will never believe so worthy a ninja was part of a plot designed by me. Such evidence will convince the Regent that I have just claims against Lord Nagamasa. He will believe that Nagamasa sent Tahishi to kill me and will not stand in my way when I seek revenge. Soon I will control the lands and wealth of Nagamasa and will be second in power to Nobunaga. And someday my power may even surpass that of the Regent."

"I am only sad," Nakamura added sarcastically, "that I will not be able to reward this worthy ninja for the great service he does me by attempting to kill me."

Tahishi was upon the first guard before he had a chance to sound an alarm. The loop of the thin wire slipped over his head and, brought tightly around his throat, cut easily through his flesh and almost severed his head from his body. A look of surprise was frozen on his face as the ninja slowly and soundlessly lowered the warrior to the ground. The tranquility of the beautiful garden had barely been disturbed.

Tahishi removed the wire and placed it around his waist under his *obi*. He paid no attention to the young, dead samurai whose blood seeped from the fine wound and soaked the earth. This death was of the past. It was no longer to be considered. He now must be concerned only with his next obstacle.

The second guard was more alert. He stood by the bridge that crossed the pond, his head moving slowly from side to side as he scanned the garden, his right hand on the hilt of his long sword. He was a large man with strong, broad shoulders. He would be a formidable opponent, Tahishi thought; one he might not be able to defeat in open combat. Guile, not strength, would be necessary to conquer this man.

Using the cypress trees for cover, Tahishi was able to move to within ten yards of the guard. The pond prevented the ninja from circling around him. And he could not approach him from the front without being seen. He would have to divert his attention and then cross those last ten yards before the samurai had a chance to recover.

The ninja undressed quickly and silently. He chose from his arsenal two *shuriken* and a razor-sharp knife, which he placed between his teeth. He braced himself against the tree that concealed him, took careful aim and sent the first *shuriken* whistling into the post of the bridge, close to the samurai's head. Startled, the guard turned in the direction of the sound, presenting the back of his head to Tahishi.

The second *shuriken* left the ninja's hand a split second later . . . and found its mark, the soft area of the neck at the base of the samurai's skull.

Tahishi was running as soon as the sharp star was in the air, his knife now held tightly in his hand. The ninja knew the *shuriken* would not kill. The initial shock would quickly pass and the samurai could recover enough to call for help. He must be stopped quickly and silently. The call must never leave his throat.

Tahishi flashed across the clearing and leaped on the samurai's back, one hand circling his head to cover his mouth, while the other hand brought the sharp blade of the knife across his throat. The samurai's body quivered violently as his life poured from the wound. He thrashed his arms wildly as he tried to drive the unseen ogre from his back, but Tahishi held on with all his might, keeping the samurai's mouth covered as his strength ebbed so that the only sound to escape his body was the low, soft gurgle of death.

Tahishi lay exhausted by the body of his second victim. He felt sharp pains across his chest and shoulders and realized that he also had suffered wounds. The *shuriken* embedded in the neck of the samurai had cut deep gashes in his body during the struggle.

He bathed his wounds in the cool water of the pond and applied the healing herbs he carried with him before he dressed. He now wished his mission was over. He would like to turn back, but he had given his pledge and had been well paid.

Moving across the bridge, Tahishi covered the distance to the palace quickly and without interference. Nakamura's bedchamber was easy to find. He was told exactly where it would be by the samurai who had paid for his services.

He crawled close to the thin wall and lay prone for many moments listening with trained ears for sound from the room. As a child, he had spent many months in seclusion in the woods and had developed so keen a sense of hearing, he could easily hear the sound of a falling leaf or of a small insect crawling on a blade of grass.

As he listened, he heard the quick breathing of someone to the left of the garden entrance to the bedchamber. It was too rapid to be the breathing of someone who was asleep. To the right, he heard the sound of the shifting of weight. There was more than one person in the room. There were other sounds, ever so slight, from other parts of the bedchamber. There were three, four, no, five people in the room. All awake. All alert. All waiting for him. It was a trap.

The number of opponents had never bothered Tahishi. He had faced and overcome greater odds on assignments in the past. But he had been prepared on those occasions. This new situation came as a complete surprise to him. He had not expected treachery. And now his mind raced for the means to complete his mission succesfully—and live.

They will be barefoot, he told himself, so as to be silent when they move. And if there is anyone occupying the bed in the room, it will not be Nakamura. He would not take such a chance, even with four men to guard him. Nakamura will be there, of course, to witness my death, but he will seek safety in the corner of the room furthest from the entrance and bed, and he will have, more than likely, his most trusted samurai by his side to defend him in case something goes wrong with his plan.

So there will be three to consider: one in the bed and one on each side of the entrance to the garden. The one in the bed will remain there, to draw my attention as I enter the room. So, the attack will come from the two at the door. I will have to deal with them first. Then I will have to dispose of the one in the bed before he has a chance to rise. The samurai guarding Nakamura will be next. And then I will deal with the great lord himself.

Reaching into the large cloth pouch that hung from his shoulder, Tahishi withdrew ten *tetsu-*

bishi, metal balls with many sharp points, each treated with a deadly poison. He arranged them in a pattern on the ground in front of the entrance.

Quietly and carefully, he then pulled himself up and under the eaves of the low roof that covered the doorway. From his *gi* top, he withdrew a thin, short reed blowgun and slipped a poison dart in one end. Placing the blowgun in his mouth and gripping it with his teeth, he then removed his short sword from the scabbard strapped to his back. There was one last step to be taken before he made his move. He slipped his knife into his right sleeve so that it would fall into his hands at the flick of his wrist.

He was now ready.

Wrapping his legs around a cedar beam in the eaves, he lowered himself until he hung with his head toward the ground and could reach the entrance panel, a foot below its top. Grasping it firmly, he let loose a blood-curdling scream through his clenched teeth and pulled the panel open.

He quickly pulled himself up as the two samurai guarding the entrance rushed into the garden to meet the intruder. All they met were the deadly poisoned *tetsu-bishi* that cut into their unprotected feet. As they screamed in agony, Tahishi swung his body down into the open doorway, hanging like a monkey by its tail, his sharp eye finding the bed and the surprised samurai propped up on his elbows in it. He grasped the blowgun held between his teeth, took quick but careful aim and sent a poisoned dart into the warrior's wide-open eye.

Somersaulting into the room, his sword in his left hand, Tahishi rolled across the floor, flicking his wrist so he could grab the point of the blade of his knife with the first two fingers and thumb of his right hand.

His sharp eyes quickly picked out Lord Nakamura in the far corner of the room cowering behind the remaining samurai. Tahishi's right arm cut the air and his knife blazed across the room and buried itself up to its hilt in the broad chest of the guard.

It was over in seconds. Four men dead or dying, and Nakamura helpless and at his mercy.

Tahishi crossed the room quickly, his short sword raised to kill. Nakamura pressed his back into the corner, searching for cover that didn't exist, his eyes wide with fear.

"You cannot kill me," he screeched. "You are in my service. It was I who paid you. I order you to lower your sword."

Tahishi smiled as he nodded toward the dead samurai sprawled at Nakamura's feet. "Your servant paid me well, and I agree I am in your service. I do accept your change of heart and will not kill you as you so ordered so that I may, in good faith, retain your fee for my services.

"But," Tahishi continued as he brought the sword down on the unprotected head of the warlord, "I have also been paid well by Lord Nagamasa, and his orders say that you must die."

APPARITION IN WHITE

It is said the gods made Japan by dipping a jeweled spear into the ocean, then holding it aloft so that the 4223 drops that fell became the Sacred Islands. Then the gods Izanagi and Izanami, learning the secret of copulation from the tadpoles, gave birth to the Japanese. From Izanagi's left eye was born Amaterasu, Goddess of the Sun, and from her grandson Ninigi sprang all the emperors of Dai Nippon.

But the emperors were not always men of strength and wisdom, and though they were called Tenshi or "Son of Heaven" and Tenno, the "Heavenly King," they were often more concerned with their own pleasures and the accumulation of fine silks and jewels than with Japan and its people.

The early Imperial Court was beautiful, the center of culture and refinement, but the land was wracked by chaos with buccaneers, pirates and bandits roaming freely without fear of retribution. As the power of the emperors faded, the strength of the lords and their clans grew mightier. Wars ravaged the land as the lords fought for power, and the islands the Chinese called "Jih-pen"— "the place from which the sun comes"—was covered by darkness.

It was during this time of war and strife that a member of the Minamoto clan, the powerful Yoritomo, gathered about him an army of many mounted samurai and vassals and established his domain. He ruled unmercifully, killing with unbridled cruelty any who didn't bend to his wishes. It is said that one of his greatest pleasures was to watch as the flesh was slowly peeled from captured samurai. The screams of the tortured men excited him, and he gave lavish rewards to those who could perform these mutilations and keep their victims alive for many hours. The longer the prisoner lived, the greater the reward.

Yoritomo was jealous of his power and feared and resented anyone in his court who was popular: A man who could win the respect and admiration of others might someday threaten his throne. Such a man, then, had to be humiliated and destroyed. He had even murdered his own brother when he suspected him of scheming against him. And one courageous samurai, who had proved his loyalty to Yoritomo in many bloody battles, but was viewed as a threat, was made to crawl naked through the streets, pulled along at the end of a rope by lowly peasants. He was then publicly castrated, tied to a post and left to die slowly as the blood dripped from his groin. He begged to be allowed the privilege of *seppuku,* but such an honorable death was denied him.

Second only to his passion for power and cruelty was his passion for young, delicate women. He had many rare beauties as concubines, but constantly looked for more. His spies would search the villages for women and bring back to the palace, often forcibly, those they knew he would enjoy.

It was on one of these searches, far from the palace, in a mountain village of fewer than one hundred people, that Yoritomo's envoys found the delicate and beautiful daughter of a blacksmith named Sasuke. She was called Shigé, and though she was only fifteen, she had fully developed as a woman. Her skin was light and soft white, her eyes shaped and colored like those of a cat, and she had a thin, straight nose and sensual lips. Overall, her bearing was aristocratic, though her nature was soft and tender. She would be, the samurai thought, a perfect catch for Yoritomo.

Sasuke was too afraid to object and Shigé was too obedient to her father to resist.

"I am deeply honored by Lord Yoritomo's choice of my unworthy daughter," the blacksmith told the envoys. "I am overjoyed that this small gift might please him. But what will I tell the merchant Seihichi. My daughter has been promised to him. . . ."

The envoy's open hand struck Sasuke across the face before he could finish.

"You can tell him he, too, has presented a gift to my master," the samurai snarled. "And if he wishes to voice his objections, we will hang his tongue as a charm around his neck."

Sasuke said nothing more as he watched his daughter silently gather her meager belongings and leave with the samurai. He did not dare touch or comfort her. When they were out of sight, he rushed to find the merchant Seihichi.

The wealthy merchant groaned when he heard

the news. A man in his middle years who had known Shigé since her birth, he had been engaged to marry her. And he had paid handsomely for her, knowing she would help bring him great prestige and enhance his position in the province. He had planned to build a fine home for her. Indeed, he had amassed a respectable fortune in his trade and had dreamed of a future of many happy years with this exciting beauty; she would have satisfied him sexually and emotionally and borne him strong sons to bring more honor and even greater prestige.

Now, all that was gone . . . torn from him by Yoritomo. There was nothing he could do but shed a tear and accept his fate. If only he had the power to strike back, to take revenge.

When his grief had lessened and reason returned, Seihichi remembered the clan of ninja he had heard about that lived in the hills a short distance from his village. Their leader, he was told, was a man of great magical power, who could turn himself into an animal or a bird, if necessary, and had performed amazing feats as an assassin and spy.

Seihichi sent word to the ninja that he had need of his services and that he would pay handsomely for them. A few days passed, and he received his reply. The ninja agreed to the meeting. But he presented conditions. He would not come to the village because there was a price on his head, and he would not risk being trapped. The merchant would have to travel to a small clearing in the forest a short distance from his home. He would have to come unarmed and alone after dark and sit on the large rock in the center of the clearing with his back to the moon. He must place be-

hind him a pouch containing one hundred taels
. . . and he must not, under any condition, turn
around.

The price of one hundred taels was a vast fortune—far more than Seihichi had been prepared
to pay—and entering the forest unarmed and
alone made his blood run cold. But his hatred for
Yoritomo was great. He agreed to all the conditions set down by the ninja.

The trees cast eerie shadows on the clearing as
Seihichi left the forest. He shivered as he crossed to
the rock, fighting to make his legs move. Each time
the wind blew, the shadows ran faster around him,
and he imagined himself surrounded by ghosts.
Though the air was cool, beads of sweat formed
on his brow, and the palms of his hands became
clammy. He took his position on the rock, placed
the pouch of money behind him as instructed and
closed his eyes to block out the fearful images
made by the trees.

Only the sound of the wind and the occasional
hoot of an owl broke the silence. Each moment
seemed an eternity, and he now regretted leaving
the safety of the village.

He shifted nervously on the rock. His hand stole
behind him to check the pouch. It was gone.

Panic seized Seihichi. He was about to turn
when he heard a voice close behind him say,
"Your money—or shall I say my money—is safe.
There is nothing to fear. Do not turn around."

The merchant began to shake uncontrollably as
the silence returned to engulf him.

"Are you still there?" Seihichi finally stuttered.

"I am here and ready to learn what you want
of me," the voice said close to his ear.

Seihichi let his grievances against Yoritomo

pour out. When he was finished, he sagged; he felt drained, weak. The devil his hatred had grown in his body was now released. It was now possessed by another.

"Yoritomo is not a man I admire or trust," the ninja said. "He has committed many crimes. Some against the people of my clan. It is time he is stopped.

"But, if he is to die, it must appear natural or by accident. If it is guessed that he has been murdered, his samurai will seek revenge. They will kill many—and you will be one of the first. They will search out all those who have recent grievances against Yoritomo. They will assume, even if they do not have evidence, that you and others are responsible. You will be tortured until you confess your guilt. And you will confess and beg to die."

Seihichi groaned and rocked his body from side to side in despair. Why had he let his hatred lead him to this terrible night.

"Do not fear." The ninja's voice was gentle and now farther away. "I will deliver your revenge to Yoritomo, and no one will ever suspect that you were involved. Be patient. It will happen soon. Now, forget this night. Strip it from your memory."

The merchant was reassured, but he had many questions.

"How will you do it? How will he die?" he asked.

. There was no answer.

"When will it happen? When?"

The only reply was the sound of the wind.

Seihichi waited and listened and then slowly turned to look behind him. There was no one there.

That same night the merchant lay in his bed and thought of his experience. Had someone really spoken to him? Had someone been in the clearing in the forest? The pouch with the money was gone, but it could have slipped from the rock and fallen to the ground. He had been too frightened to look around him before he fled from the woods back to his home. Was his mind beset by devils? He would just have to wait and see.

Yoritomo looked at the sleeping Shigé and was pleased. She had given him great pleasure this month she had been with him. She was a jewel . . . one that would become more lustrous and valuable with time. He would remember to give an extra reward to the samurai who found her.

The evening was warm. He walked to the garden; night sounds soothed him. He closed his eyes and breathed deeply.

"You seem well and happy, brother."

The voice hissed and echoed as if coming from a cave.

Yoritomo shivered. "Who is it? Who speaks to me?"

"Do you forget your brother, your faithful, devoted brother?"

A chill sped up Yoritomo's spine as his eyes raced across the garden, searching the darkness.

"I wait for you, brother. I wait for you to join me."

Yoritomo turned and rushed back into his chamber. He did not believe the dead return, but he had heard the voice, and it did sound as if it came from the grave. But it could not have been. It was a dream, he reasoned. He would sleep. It would be forgotten.

But Yoritomo did not forget, and a week later, after drinking heavily and dropping off to sleep as if he was drugged, he was awakened by the sound of dragging feet. He fought to open his heavy eyes as he heard the mournful moans. He could barely raise his head, and his vision was clouded, but he saw in the darkness before him a figure covered from the top of its head to the floor by a long white robe. His head reeled, and he felt as if he was in the middle of a dense fog. He could not move or utter a sound. He finally forced his hand to move until he found the handle of his sword, but he was too weak to lift it.

"Do you wish to kill me again?" the voice called from the darkness.

Yoritomo groaned and closed his eyes.

"I come for you, dear brother. I come to take you before the gods for judgment. You have killed me, one of your own blood, and you must now pay the penalty."

Yoritomo began to whimper, then collapsed.

Yoritomo's retainers were concerned about their master. Black rings circled his heavy eyes. He drank his sake with shaking hands. And he drank much more than they had ever seen him consume before. He was startled by the slightest noise and flew into violent rages for little or no reason. He shunned his food and the attention of his concubines. And he became obsessed with death and talked of it constantly. Though he never spoke of his experiences for fear of being thought mad, he did call together learned teachers of his realm to question them about the one hundred twenty-eight hells and the world of demons.

As his condition worsened, Yoritomo spent more and more time by himself in contemplation or on rides in the woods of his estate just before dawn. His brother had appeared before him twice more, awakening him from a drugged sleep as before, and now he was certain the dead were able to return to haunt the living.

His samurai watched him carefully though discreetly, keeping him in their sight whenever possible because of their fear that he might do himself harm.

On his morning rides, his retainers would follow at a distance so as not to disturb their master, and although they were often in plain view, Yoritomo never showed any signs that he saw them. He would begin his rides at a slow trot. The farther he got from the castle, the faster he rode, until his strong horse was at full gallop, and the wind ripped at his face and stung his eyes.

He avoided the road and tore through the woods, leaping over fallen trees and narrow streams, ending his ride atop a steep hill strewn with loose rocks that avalanched to the gully below as his horse struggled up the perilous incline. The animal slipped and strained, and when it reached the top it glistened with sweat, and white foam covered its mouth. It shuddered, snorted and pawed the ground as Yoritomo sat straight in his saddle and watched the early sun rise in the east.

For a moment Yoritomo felt free of his devil and cleansed of the evil that tore at his soul.

The warlord would return to the palace slowly, fearful of the ghosts that awaited him . . . fearful of the nightmares he knew were more than dreams.

Two weeks passed without the appearance of the ghostly figure of his brother, and the warlord hoped this was a sign that his trial had ended. His spirits rose, and he once again lay with Shigé, attacking her fragile body as a starving man attacks a feast.

When fully satisfied, he sent her away and drank sake until he fell asleep.

And then it happened.

Just before dawn, he was awakened by something cold touching his cheek. His body trembled as he slowly opened his eyes. There, standing above him, was the apparition in white, the rusted sword in his hand touching Yoritomo's face. It was his brother's sword, the same weapon that had been placed in his grave to placate his soul. Yoritomo closed his eyes and prayed for deliverance. The cold left his cheek, and when he finally gathered strength to open his eyes, the figure was gone.

Yoritomo struggled to his feet, dressed himself with trembling hands and rushed to his stables. He kicked his groom awake and ordered his horse saddled. Muttering incoherently about the demons that were after him, he mounted and rode at full gallop into the woods.

He screamed curses to the sky as branches tore through his garments and flesh. The horse seemed to sense the danger and ran as fast as it could, passing through the forest like a storm. The chest of the animal heaved and breath poured in great clouds from its nostrils as it began the climb up the rocky hill. Yoritomo urged the horse on with threats and kicks. The rocks flew and broke beneath its hooves.

Suddenly, just before the top, a blood-curdling scream ripped the air. Yoritomo raised his eyes and saw before him on the peak the apparition in white, the rusted sword raised above its head!

The frightened horse reared and lost its footing on the loose rocks, tumbling down the hill with Yoritomo still in the saddle, ending at the bottom with the warlord pinned beneath its great body.

Yoritomo died a few months later at the age of fifty-three. He spent his last days babbling about the ghost of his brother. His death was attributed to the demons he had offended. Only the merchant Seihichi suspected it was not a spirit of the dead but a living, cunning ninja who had killed the great lord.

THE WARNING

The tall samurai entered the tiny village east of Kyoto on the island of Honshu. His *ayigasa*, a rush hat lined with silk, was pulled over his brow and cast a shadow over his eyes and most of his face. His light-colored hunting garment was in sharp contrast to the shining black-lacquered scabbard of the sword worn on his left side.

He moved silently, cautiously. But his stride was confident; his bearing arrogant. His eyes flicked along the tiny huts that lined the quiet road. The villagers were nowhere to be seen, though he felt eyes following him as he moved past the homes. They had taken refuge from the sun, but they would have gone inside even on a cloudy day to avoid contact with this mysterious warrior.

The samurai was satisfied. He did not want to meet anyone who might delay his finding the artist, Hirata. The orders from his master, a most trusted *daimyo* of the regent Hideyoshi, were explicit: He must quickly find Hirata and convince him, by any means he found suitable, that he must surrender his beautiful daughter, Okane, to the palace at Edo. She would be a gift to the powerful Hideyoshi and would bring great honor and favor to his master. The samurai was warned he would not be allowed the privilege of an honorable death if he failed. Instead, he would be banished to Korea, where he would join Hideyoshi's army in its futile attempt to conquer that mysterious peninsula. He would serve as the lowliest of soldiers and surely suffer an ignominious death.

The samurai was not worried about his fate, because he was sure he would not fail. The villagers were frightened and unarmed. And Hirata was an old man. He would have no trouble completing his mission successfully.

Still, he had been warned that Hirata was not a man to be taken lightly. He was a ninja, a member of the clan that had harassed the forces of Hideyoshi as they traveled from Edo to Kyoto before they had been overwhelmed by the great might of the ruling regent. It was rumored that he had caused many deaths in horrible, devious ways and was only allowed to live because Hideyoshi was not anxious to continue this draining war against these terrifying peasants at a time when he was so involved with other, more important campaigns. He would return to them later, when his warriors returned from Korea, and wipe them out. Meanwhile, there would be peace . . . a peace of hatred and distrust.

A smile crossed the samurai's face as he recalled his meeting with a merchant who knew Hirata. It was at an inn fifty miles from the village. He had shared sake with the fat, jovial merchant who was relaxed by the polite, unimportant conversation and mellowed by the wine. It was then that the samurai brought up the subject of Hirata. Did the merchant know him? Did he know where he lived? Did he know of his habits? Did he know the powers he possessed? The merchant nodded yes to all the questions.

"I do not wish to know why you seek Hirata," the merchant said. "I fear the knowledge would be dangerous. As dangerous as Hirata can be. Do not be fooled by his age and quiet manner. Hirata is a devious man, as all ninja are devious men. He has mastered the use of poisons, so you must not accept any food or drink he offers you. And do not let him touch you. It has been said that he conceals in his hands needles coated with poison of deadly potency. Though you are young and strong, he will prove to be a worthy opponent, if you seek him as an opponent.

"He lives at the far end of the village, in a home on a knoll bordered by a small stream. He lives with his daughter, Okane, the most beautiful flower to grow on Honshu, who serves and honors him as if he was a mighty lord. He lives peacefully now, working on his art from dawn to dark. But don't be deceived by this serenity. He is dangerous. He is devious."

The samurai was satisfied by the information he received from the drunken merchant, and now, as he approached the tiny house on the knoll, he was confident he would succeed with his mission.

The samurai had to lower his head to look through the open door of the home of Hirata. Because of the blinding glare of the midday sun, it took a few moments for his eyes to become accustomed to the shaded room. It was simply furnished . . . almost barren. A few *tatami* on the floor, a tea service of simple design on a low table in the middle of the room, a stove and cooking utensils in the far corner. A lamp hung from the ceiling, but provided little illumination. Most of the far wall was open to a small, well-kept garden of rocks and trees. In the center of the opening, silhouetted in the light, a small figure sat cross-legged at a low table. He was, the samurai saw, painting with brush and ink, and he was so intent with his work, he didn't see, or seemed not to see, the tall figure in the doorway.

"I seek the man called Hirata." The voice of the samurai boomed with authority.

The figure slowly straightened at the table and, without turning, answered.

"I am Hirata. How can I be of service to you?"

The samurai entered the room, throwing back his shoulders and appearing even more massive than he really was. He approached Hirata with strong strides. He would impress the artist with his power immediately. He was now confident there would be no trouble.

"I am from Mito, and I bring an offer that will honor your house."

Hirata rose slowly and turned. He was slender and much taller than he appeared when seated. He wore a *hakama* over his simple white kimono. His hair was full and long, touched with gray. A small beard barely covered the point of his chin. The samurai was astonished that the face of the artist was unlined, that his eyes were clear and youthful. But he was most impressed by Hirata's hands. They did not seem to fit his body. They were large and powerful . . . the hands of a man of great strength . . . of a warrior.

"You already do me honor by entering my

humble home," Hirata said as he bowed slightly, his hands clasped before him.

The samurai did not return the bow. He would establish immediately who was the superior, even if it meant insulting his host. Hirata did not seem to notice or simply ignored the rudeness.

"I offer you tea. Or perhaps you would prefer sake," he said, pointing toward the table in the middle of the room.

The samurai declined. He moves quickly, he thought.

"I am eager to return quickly to Mito with your gift to my master, the Lord Hideyoshi," the samurai said as he pushed his hat back so it hung on his back by the string that had held it under his chin. Hirata looked calmly at his face. It was a cruel, coarse face; deep, evil eyes were separated by a wide nose. The chin was square and strong, and blue shadow barely hid cheeks ravaged by the pox. This is a man who has killed many with little remorse, Hirata thought. And with the slightest provocation, he will kill again.

"I am flattered that you believe I have something worthy of a gift to the great Hideyoshi," Hirata said humbly. "But as you can see, this is a simple house. I have simple possessions. And my art is of mediocre quality, more suitable for burning than as a gift."

The samurai eyed Hirata coldly. He is a shrewd man. I don't know how he has learned, but he knows why I am here. Let us now see if he is as courageous as he is shrewd.

The samurai drew his sword and placed it against the cheek of the artist. With only the slightest pressure, he made a small cut. Hirata remained stationary and soundless as blood dribbled down his chin and dripped onto his white kimono.

"I do not want your crude art or your simple possessions," the samurai growled. "The gift I come for is your daughter. Bring her to me immediately."

Hirata stared without apparent emotion at the samurai, but as the sword was raised, he clapped his hands twice, and a young girl entered from the garden. She was the loveliest girl the samurai had ever seen: a small, delicate figure, barely in her teens, with skin that was almost transparent, perfect features, a comely figure. She was indeed a worthy prize for any king. His master would be pleased and reward him handsomely.

"You act with wisdom, if not with honor or courage," the samurai sneered. "I pay for your gift with your life. Come, Okane, I take you to a far better life. A life of service to our Lord Hideyoshi."

With his sword still drawn, the samurai took the fightened Okane by the hand and led her to the door. She offered no resistance and did not look at her father, who hadn't moved or uttered a sound. At the door, the samurai turned to Hirata.

"Now would be a good time for you to enjoy some of your tea and sake." He sheathed his sword and strode triumphantly down the village road with Okane running to keep up with him.

The inn was almost deserted when the samurai entered with Okane. He surveyed the large room from the door, a caution that had become a habit on all his missions. He was drained by the constant vigilance he had had to keep since leaving Hirata's home and wanted nothing more than a good meal, something to drink and a little rest. He was pleased to see the merchant he had met on his previous visit having his meal of rice and boiled fish in the far corner. Their eyes met and the merchant smiled and motioned for the samurai to join him.

The samurai sat wearily on the thin *tatami* spread before the table and hungrily gulped the cup of sake offered to him by the merchant. Okane sat sullenly at his side, her eyes lowered and puffed with unshed tears.

"I thank you for your hospitality and the helpful advice you gave me when we last met. I toast your health and your future," the samurai said, and he drained the second cup of sake.

Now that he was seated he felt the weariness spread through his body. He felt light-headed, as if he had drunk too much. But then his arms felt leaden, his legs throbbed and a searing pain tore across his chest. The merchant was smiling and speaking to him, but he had to strain to hear what he was saying.

"Hirata thanks you for your gift of life. To repay you he will now remove the burden of his unworthy daughter from your tired shoulders. He is sorry you saw fit to reject his hospitality on your visit to his home. He knows it was an oversight on your part and has sent his favorite sake to soothe and warm you."

The merchant rose and taking Okane by the hand walked slowly to the door. The samurai sat paralyzed, unable to stop him.

"I warned you," the merchant said as he went out the door. "Hirata is a devious man. All of us ninja are devious men."

I AM NINJA!

The scene just north of the city of Nora was one of tranquil beauty. It was twilight and the horizon, backdrop to the gently rolling hills, was brownish, colored like the edge of an old page. The few clouds in the pale beige sky had their undersides brushed with pink.

The servants and hirelings flanking the dirt road just outside the impressive castle gate seemed tranquil and happy, too, as they watched their lord and master Matsumo Nakabayshi approach on horseback. A double line of samurai behind him, also mounted, raised a cloud of dust.

But appearances were deceiving. The people were not happy, tranquil. Matsumo Nakabayshi's appearance was enough to start the worm of fear in anyone's belly. A large gruff man with what looked like a jovial face from afar, he was scary up close, his black eyes mean and constantly shifting, looking for the slightest glimmer of disrespect.

If he found it, his wrath was swift. With stomach-sickening ferocity he would have the head of the culprit—or supposed culprit—lopped off and ingloriously mounted on one of the fence posts around the compound.

Now, as he came, his eyes seemed not to miss a single one of all those smiling, obsequious faces. Faces of people who wanted to live.

The boy standing among those who flanked the road was named Hashiro Seiko. He was twelve years old. He smiled into the black eyes of Nakabayshi as he went by, and bowed.

Hashiro hoped two things. That Nakabayshi had noticed him, but had not detected what was behind the smiling eyes. If he had, the boy would have been summarily decapitated.

Both wishes seemed to be granted. Immediately after passing, Nakabayshi turned and said something to the samurai directly behind him and pointed to Hashiro. The samurai wheeled his horse out of line, dismounted and walked to the boy. The samurai looked down with a slight, knowing smile on his face and said:

"Be at Lord Nakabayshi's quarters tonight at eight."

Those around knew, too. Hashiro was handsome; slim but solidly built. He was to be a *chigo* for Nakabayshi, a boy whore.

It had started six months before, the day like any other day Hashiro had spent with his father, a *genin* in the Yamamoto Ryu, since he had reached his sixth birthday: It was a day of training to become a ninja.

First they had run, then exercised, then breakfasted on green tea, rice balls and raw fish. The day gave Hashiro pleasure, even though his father was a stern taskmaster. It was a pleasure to be a ninja, like his father.

At around ten-thirty, as was also the custom, Hashiro had carried the two empty oak buckets to a stream not far from their home to get water. He filled the buckets, then started back over the gently hilly terrain toward the house.

He was halfway back when he heard the sound. At first he thought it was his mother and sister, who were away visiting an uncle, but then he remembered that they were not due back for another week.

He pondered who it could be, but had no answer. He would find out soon enough, he thought, as he approached a final hillock that overlooked his home.

Wait! It was a sense his father had taught him. A sense beyond the five senses. A sense that something was awry. Something wrong.

Hashiro stopped just short of the crest of the hillock and, controlling his breathing so he wouldn't be heard and carefully lowering the buckets, lowered himself and peered over the edge, his presence hidden by rock outcroppings.

It took everything Hashiro had learned about containing himself to keep from crying out. The area in front of the plain-board gray shack of his father, which was bare packed earth, teemed with mounted samurai in full, colorful, armored battle dress. Standing between two clusters of the *bushi* was his father, still bare-chested and in the shorts he had on during training, and a warlord. With spreading alarm Hashiro realized that the warlord was Nakabayshi, whom his father had once pointed out in the village and about whom there were legions of stories concerning his cruelty and savagery.

All was quiet, except for the movement and occasional snorting of the horses and the gruff, throaty voice of Nakabayshi, who was castigating his father for something. There was, Hashiro knew, no way that Nakabayshi could know that his father was ninja, but he was disturbed by something else. He knew his father. No matter what the odds, he would fight. And die.

It happened suddenly, as if the samurai knew Hashiro's father would fight given the chance. Two came behind him and grabbed him, and then two more. They turned him around while Nakabayshi did something with his own clothes.

Hashiro realized what was going to be done just as the samurai forced his father to bend over at the waist and one stripped his shorts down to his knees. Then Nakabayshi appoached, his own trousers down by his knees.

Hashiro's father made no sound as it was happening to him nor, as he had been taught all these years, did Hashiro. But the boy could not control the bitter taste of bile followed by the surge of vomit. . . .

Hashiro came down after the samurai had left. His father was standing in the kitchen. His eyes were dark and sad, but there was a special light in them.

He approached the boy and touched his cheek. "You did well, my son. You are now ninja, and I am not concerned with you anymore."

For a moment their eyes locked, and the boy was on the verge of saying something. But he knew there was nothing to say.

The boy felt a weakening as his father turned

and left him, walking toward the bedroom. Hashiro went outside and looked up at the sky. It was a powder blue with clear, fleecy clouds in it. They blurred. Tears filled his eyes, burned, rolled down on his cheeks.

His heart stopped. From inside the house he heard the brief savage cry of his father. No one was around. Hashiro was alone. He fell to his knees, his small heart bursting with agony. He was not ninja.

He was a boy.

Two days after his father had been buried—and the death had been the result of a disagreement over taxes—Hashiro was back in training, this time under the tutelage of his uncle. Other ninja of the *ryu* had immediately plotted revenge on Nakabayshi, but the boy had steadfastly refused.

"I," he said, "will avenge the spirit of my father."

No one knew it was a lie, but it was. From the moment his father had died, all the groundwork of all the years had gone from Hashiro. He no longer felt like ninja.

But he kept up the appearance of ninja for his mother and sister. He was the only man now, and they needed him to be strong.

Each night he would proceed to the hill where his father's spirit had been buried and talk with him. Talk with him and say he was sorry.

But mostly he would cry. Tears that came from somewhere bottomless and empty. He cried for his father and their life. And he cried, too, because he had promised to avenge his father's spirit against Nakabayshi, and yet he knew he would not. He was afraid. He was twelve years old and afraid.

Many men had died trying to assassinate Naka-bayshi. How could he possibly succeed?

Then one night, for the briefest of moments, he considered *seppuku*. A quick, deep pull across his abdomen and it would be over, all over.

And in that moment he also had an idea. His tears ceased and were replaced by something else: a small white-hot pinpoint of flame. A flame of revenge that would never turn off until Nakabay-shi was dead.

But how? Hashiro knew many things, but there was a central fact to consider. He was twelve, Nakabayshi was clever and alert to assassination attempts, and he was well protected by some of the best and fiercest samurai in Japan.

Still, Hashiro thought, during all those years, all those days, father taught me much. I know much, too.

Early on in the development of his plan, Hashiro decided that he had at least one very good factor on his side: He did not care if the attempt on Nakabayshi's life would cost him his own. His father, taking from the teachings of the great warrior Miyamoto Musashi, had taught him that: If you already consider yourself dead, you will not know fear and will do things that ordinary men will not. . . .

Two months before he stood on the side of the road outside Nakabayshi's fortress, Hashiro began. He made his way, deep in the night, to a narrow street at a far end of the village. He stopped in front of a house which looked like all the others and tapped on the lacquered front door.

Almost immediately the door opened and a thin woman of indeterminate age, her face heavily coated with cosmetics and wearing a silk kimono, looked at Hashiro quizzically.

"I am here to see the woman Yokio," he said.

The woman looking at him was a madam, a feudal geisha, and she had seen much that was bizarre in her time. Still, she had started to smile at the sight of a young boy at her brothel; but Yokio's name had stopped the smile, and she had narrowed her eyes suspiciously.

"What do you want with her?"

"I want her as a woman."

"That can't be anymore."

"I know all about her," Hashiro said, "and I will pay well." From inside his shirt Hashiro withdrew a *tachi,* a short sword. The eyes of the madam dilated. Even in the light from the oil lamps she could make out glints of green on the *tsuka,* or handle. Emeralds. And the blade was etched and decorated.

"I will give you this," the boy said.

Wordlessly, the madam took the sword and led the boy into the interior of the brothel. A sweet yet acrid smell permeated the air: opium and perfume.

He padded down a long, dim corridor flanked by closed doorways. Occasionally, Hashiro could hear the soft tinkle of laughter from behind the closed doors.

He went down more corridors where there were no doors and no laughter and was left standing by the madam in front of a door that was badly in need of lacquer. He entered.

The room, which was fairly well lit by an oil lamp, was heavy wtih the smell of opium. He closed the door behind him.

The woman, Yokio, was sitting on the floor

among pillows. In one hand she held a clay pipe which she sucked on intermittently.

Unlike the madam, or the rest of the prostitutes in the house, Yokio, whom the boy judged to be about thirty, was without makeup. Indeed, all she wore was a pair of silken shorts.

She looked up at Hashiro and smiled, revealing rotten teeth. Her large, dark eyes were wild, glazed; a little spittle ran from one corner of her mouth. It was not the opium. Yokio was hopelessly insane.

It was just what Hashiro had overheard one day. It was what he had hoped.

Hashiro sat on a polished oak bench outside the bedroom of Matsumo Nakabayshi, warlord supreme. It was ten minutes to eight.

The boy had prepared himself well. He had bathed carefully, cleaned his nails, brushed back his shiny crop of black hair. He wore a light, green silken kimono, pulled tight at the waist. It accented the sleek lines of his body, his burgeoning manhood.

Convulsive emotions pecked at the edge of his consciousness. Errant thoughts. Of how girls, young girls, in the *ryu* used to laugh and giggle when they saw him. The hard, dark, angry eyes of his father as he corrected him for doing this or that wrong, but the light of love behind those eyes. The specter of his father, dishonored, abused, his abdomen drenched with red. Tears on the face of his mother, twin rivers of sorrow in the sun of an afternoon. Yokio, mad, not knowing what was happening, the stench of her strong, forcing himself to go on.

And then, just after he had wheedled his way

into the stable boy job here, the day he left his mother, he knew from her eyes that she realized it could be for the last time. But she held her tears and grasped him firmly, and he could feel the beating of her heart.

Hashiro blinked, gathered himself up to concentrate. It was what father had taught. Forget all but what you do. Throw out pain, sorrow, fear, all . . . live within the moment and for the moment and you will succeed.

He felt it before he heard it. Movement inside the room. And then the rice paper panel slid open, and a big samurai emerged.

Hashiro calculated that he had done the right thing, and it was confirmed by the samurai's action. He made the boy strip, then carefully searched him. If Hashiro had brought a weapon —he had considered taping a needle dipped in puffer poison to the sole of his foot—he would have been discovered. It was becoming clear why Nakabayshi stayed alive and so many of his enemies were dead.

The search completed, the boy was instructed to put his kimono back on and was led into the room. Nakabayshi, dressed only in shorts, was sitting on the floor eating rice with chopsticks.

He smiled when he saw Hashiro. The boy was obviously to his liking. He would be a good *chigo*.

"Sit down next to me," Nakabayshi said, and Hashiro obeyed. As he did, he noticed that hanging on the wall, as he had hoped, just six feet away, was a *katana* in its scabbard.

Hashiro let his eyes just touch the *katana* and then turned his attention to Nakabayshi.

Nakabayshi, piggishly stuffing the rice into his mouth, his jowels greasy, spoke to Hashiro, asking him what he did on the compound, where he was from. It was all idle preamble. Lust was in the air.

As Nakabayshi talked, a strange thing happened to Hashiro. He stopped feeling like a boy. He started to feel, and then fully felt, like a man. And he would act like a man. A ninja.

Later, as he lay next to Nakabayshi, he thought only of the *katana* hanging in its scabbard on the wall.

Nabakayshi was asleep, his breathing jerky, like someone really asleep rather than someone feigning it.

Hashiro had a decision to make. To leap quickly for the *katana,* or to employ stealthy step, *nuki ashi.*

He decided on the latter. Effortlessly, silently, he raised himself up and walked quietly across the rush mat, toward the *katana.*

It was the rush mat which defeated him. He did not see the only fractionally loose board beneath it, and when he stepped on it the sound figuratively exploded in the room.

Hashiro knew that he had only an instant. In one stride he was to the *katana* and had withdrawn it with a wicked whoosh and turned. In the side of his eye he saw the samurai burst through the door, and let loose with a savage cry.

Nakabayshi was on the ground, and the boy raised the *katana* and chopped downward at the fat, loathsome figure. But the figure was moving and the sword missed, embedding itself deeply in the wood so that the boy could not withdraw it again.

"No!" Nakabayshi cried as the samurai brought

his own *katana* up, ready to decapitate the boy.
"No."

Hashiro went into *hira no kamae,* ready for
battle, but soon the room was filled with samurai.
They quickly overpowered him, held him fast.
Held him as his father was held that seemingly
long time ago.

Nakabayshi approached. His face was sweaty,
smiling, but his eyes were black beads of savagery.

"Why do you want to kill me, little *chigo*? And
how could you expect to when so many have
failed?"

The warlord turned to leave the room, stopped,
turned at the doorway.

"Now," he said, "we are going to have some
fun with you. You should have succeeded. Never
strike a king, my boy, unless you can kill him."

Nakabayshi turned, but Hashiro's words stopped
him. Hashiro spoke, feeling the fullness of ninja
heritage in himself.

"But I have killed you, great sir. You are dead
but don't know it. And you will die more horribly
than anyone you have ever killed."

Nakabayshi let out a guttural laugh, and all the
other samurai in the room laughed with him.

Later, they skinned Hashiro alive. But through
the red welter of his pain which, at one point, he
became insensitive to, as if pain was its own an-
esthetic, he rejoiced. He had succeeded, and he
would be joining the spirit of his father very soon!

And four months after this, when Nakabayshi
got the note that had been covertly delivered, he
understood what was wrong with him, why he
could not walk straight, why his body had erupted
with sores and why, three weeks after he had been

with the chigo, a sore had appeared on his genitals and then healed.

The note read:

When you read this I will be dead. I will either have died by your hand, or I will be dead from the geisha disease I contracted at a brothel in Nora some time ago. The geisha disease that I contracted in case I failed to kill you in another way.

First, you should know a sore will appear on your privates, but then go away. Then your body will break out in rashes and various eruptions, and you will feel sicker and sicker and weaker and weaker. Finally, it will drive you insane. Insane because bugs get inside the brain, and insane with pain.

You will then hope that one of your enemies finishes you off.

Hashiro Seiko

But Nakabayshi didn't wait that long. A few days after receiving Hashiro's note Nakabayshi committed *seppuku*. He left no note.

THE TRAP

Fuozo Hakido, regent of the Toga Prefecture, sat cross-legged on a rush mat and drank sake from an incongruously small cup. Opposite him, also seated, was his wife, Meiko. It was early evening of a warm spring day, and they were in one of the rear rooms of one of the many buildings and fortifications which comprised the warlord's compound.

Hakido enjoyed looking at Meiko. Since the moment he had seen her a little over two years before, he had thought her the most beautiful woman he had ever seen, and no woman he had seen since had negated that thought. Now, in the half light, she seemed lovelier than ever. Her skin seemed only slightly paler than the snow-white kimono she was wearing, and her dark hair and dark liquid eyes formed a startling but pleasing contrast. Her figure was full, firm, ripe.

Hakido poured himself more sake. He was slightly drunk and felt a stirring in his loins. Tonight, he thought, would be special.

Meiko recognized the slightly glazed look in Hakido's eyes. It was a look of lust. Tonight, she knew, they would be pillowing. It was not a thought she savored.

And there was something else, some other glimmer in the dark eyes set in the ruddy, pockmarked face that she couldn't quite define but did not like. It was a look, she thought, that she had seen before, akin to the one Hakido would have when watching his enemies tortured and executed. A look of sadistic pleasure.

Hakido spoke. His eyes seemed glassier, the lids heavy, the lips disgustingly wet.

"The day after tomorrow," he said, "we take Kyotu. Right in Torinara's backyard."

Kyotu was a town about forty miles from the compound in land occupied by Lord Torinara, who had been warring with Hakido for three years and whose military fortunes had been steadily increasing. What Meiko hadn't known and what made her adrenaline surge and her heart jump, though her face remained tranquil, was that an attack was planned, on the town it was planned, and when. For two years Meiko had lived with this son of a sow, but it was data like these which made it all worthwhile, that blotted out the sour taste of sake from his mouth, all the bloody executions and torture she had witnessed. Indeed, doubly worthwhile in this instance. The information on Kyotu would give Lord Torinara a military advantage over Hakido and, particularly appealing, save lives. When Hakido arrived with his bloodthirsty hordes to sack the town, everybody would be gone, warned off by Torinara, who would likely wait in ambush.

"I wish you luck, my lord," Meiko said, smiling

at the image of the empty village and the expression on Hakido's face.

Hakido nodded and smiled back.

Later, as she suspected, they pillowed. Tonight it seemed different. Hakido had never been a gentle lover, but tonight he was rough, almost savage, but after a few torturous minutes it was over. Hakido, sleepily drunk, immediately rolled over. Much later Meiko fell asleep. Something, she thought, was wrong.

It was the early hours of the morning when Hakido awoke again. He smiled in the darkness. The trap had been baited, the hook neatly hidden.

Hakido was almost sure that the trap would net him a spy—his wife. Or, more properly, a *kunoichi*—a whore of a female ninja spy . . .

Eighteen months earlier, when she had started feeding espionage information to Lord Torinara, Meiko and the lord had established a virtually undetectable communications link. Some fifty yards outside the perimeter of Hakido's compound was a dense forest. Unobserved, stylus and rice paper secreted in her garment, Meiko would walk to a certain tree in the forest. She would write the message, then place it in a hole in the tree. Later that night, a ninja would pick up the communication and take it to Torinara.

The information was always "transmitted" at the last possible moment simply because it could change. Natural factors, weather chiefly, could interfere with Hakido's plans; and he sometimes changed them for no apparent reason. Meiko wanted to ensure that the information was as accurate as possible.

Meiko's most valuable tool for determining the

accuracy of information she had received from Hakido was the acquaintanceships she had carefully developed with the highest-ranking samurai in Hakido's army. Hakido would notify these men of his plans or any changes.

The next day she made it a point to accidentally meet Yukio Ochi, a general in the army and a tall, handsome man who always seemed a little discomfited by her presence.

She met him in one of the many garden areas of the compound. It was a pleasant day, and she took the opportunity to make small talk about it and eventually slipped into the main business at hand.

"And where," she said, "are you off to today?"

"No place today," Ochi said. "Today we prepare. Tomorrow we march."

"Oh," Meiko said, her face beaming innocently, "and where will you be going?"

"I don't know," the samurai said.

Meiko's brow almost furrowed. She was puzzled. But she kept her tone flat.

"Oh. My Lord didn't tell you?"

"No," Ochi said, "Lord Hakido said he was not sure yet what course he would follow. Except that it will be tomorrow."

Like all ninja, male or female, Meiko's sense of danger was acute. Now she sensed it and felt her palms getting damp. Suddenly, she had to be by herself. She bowed, smiled and left Ochi as quickly as she could. She only half-noticed that he seemed reluctant to have her leave.

Slowly, she walked between the sculptured designs and rows of flowers, the image of beauty, decorum and womanly grace. But inside, her system was in turmoil, her *kunoichi* mind working furiously.

Now she understood the strange gleam in Hakido's eye. It was the look of a cat playing with a rat. He had set a trap for her. She had been the only one he had told about Kyotu, because if Ochi didn't know, nobody did. Now, if she warned Torinara of Hakido's impending raid on Kyotu, and he warned the people and Hakido showed up at an empty village, he would know that it was because of information she provided—there could be no one else.

She might escape with her life. Might. But the espionage network she had had set up would be over—a network which she had worked on for three years, from the time she had first arranged a meeting with Hakido, to becoming his paramour, to becoming his wife.

It was an espionage network that had worked on his kingdom like a cancer. Indeed, Torinara himself had told her that her contribution to his cause had been crucially important. And how would its end affect the cause? It would hurt it badly. Hakido's army was much larger than Torinara's and it was espionage and cleverness that often made up for manpower and swords.

Meiko stopped, almost involuntarily.

For a moment, she considered not communicating anything to Torinara. Maybe Hakido would do nothing to the town. Maybe it was just a test of her.

No, he would. Hakido made bloodshed an end in itself. If she said nothing, the dusty streets of Kyotu would run red.

She started walking again. And would that be so bad? Lives would be lost, many lives. But her position would be intact, perhaps stronger than ever once she had passed Hakido's test.

All she would have to do, she knew, was forget the images of Kyotu, the images that were bound to materialize. Of old people being beheaded, of children committing unspeakable acts, of young men forced to commit *seppuku* by some of the more sadistic samurai in Hakido's army.

That's all.

And then she remembered something else. What was the fight for? Why had she originally joined the forces of Torinara against Hakido? Why had she left her mother with tears streaming down her face, her brothers and sisters saying their sad goodbyes, perhaps forever?

She had done it because Torinara represented what was good and just in feudal Japan. He was not a man possessed by a craze for power or land or money. He had come out of the mountains of Iga to make war on Hakido because he, Torinara, was a man obsessed with justice. Not that he was gentle. He could be a ruthless killer, a clever tactician, a brutal enemy. But beneath the iron of his character was a heart—a heart which led him along a path that was right. He would do much, but he would not let these people of Kyotu die for the cause. There would be a better way or there would be no way.

And, finally, the realization: It was not really her decision to make! It stuck in her throat, but she was a soldier in Torinara's army, not the general. She would merely tell him what had occurred, then follow what course he took.

Before she went back to her living quarters, Meiko picked up a writing implement and some paper and took a leisurely walk to the woods.

There, out of sight, she wrote the message briefly, telling Torinara of Kyotu, and the trap that Hakido had laid for her. If possible, she asked him to send her instructions on what to do, though she had no idea how he would do it, granted his distance from the compound and the fact that the march to Kyotu would begin early in the morning.

Hakido was even drunker and rougher than the previous night, and Meiko found herself controlling her instinct, with some degree of difficulty, to simply kill him. But he fell asleep even faster than he had the night before.

Meiko found that she could not sleep. It occurred to her that tomorrow she would be dead. If she knew Hakido, he would ask her to accompany him to Kyotu. There, he would see the abandoned village and know. Then he would take action.

Meiko had seen Hakido take action once before on a suspected spy, also a woman, though not a *kunoichi*. First he had her stripped and thrown to the samurai. She was then gang raped, half boiled alive and then, when mercy no longer mattered, beheaded.

But that would not happen to her. As she approached the town she would slip out the specially prepared cyanide pill—a core of deadly cyanide covered with dough. She would have it swallowed and be dead before Hakido could react. She would commit *jigai* in her own style. She would die the death of a warrior.

Still, to live . . . living was a bird in the sky, laughter of a loved one on a summer night. Living was . . .

Meiko cut herself off. She was a *kunoichi*. She had taken that path long ago. Now, like a true warrior, she must walk it to the end, whatever that might be.

The day dawned bright and clear, a high sun in a cloudless blue sky.

As she suspected, Hakido, now barely concealing his hostility, told her to accompany him on the march to Kyotu. They started out, hundreds of mounted samurai in battle dress, *daisho* clanking.

Hakido instructed her to ride beside him. As they went he made sly inquiries as to how she was feeling. But his eyes belied his concern. They burned into her.

As they went, and despite herself, Meiko found herself getting depressed. It was, she thought, a very unwarriorlike way to act, but it was the way she felt. She only hoped that she had the courage to see it through.

Five miles, she estimated, into the march, Hakido brought what he was thinking out in the open. It had apparently been simmering in him, for he turned, his face florid:

"You are a spy," he said softly and malevolently, "aren't you?"

Meiko had no chance to answer and wondered why Hakido's mouth was open yet he was saying nothing. And then she understood the soft whoosh she had heard as he finished the sentence: There was the bloody point of an arrow sticking out of his Adam's apple. And then quickly, whoosh . . . whoosh . . . whoosh . . . whoosh . . . his body suddenly became a pincushion, but instead of pins there were arrows sticking out of him . . .

Shouts and cries, yelling, arrows rained in. They had been passing through a hilly portion of the prefecture—a perfect spot for ambush.

The fight lasted all of five minutes, a brief skirmish, but many samurai were killed and even the horse of Meiko had been shot out from under her.

Hakido was examined by a doctor for the army and was declared dead. A decision was made: Return to camp. . . .

Yukio Ochi, the handsome samurai, succeeded Hakido. After a respectable period of mourning he married the bereaved widow, Meiko. And six months later, in good part because of the continuing espionage activities of Meiko, Lord Torinara conquered the Prefecture of Toga and for years ruled with wisdom and justice.

Sometimes, Meiko would reflect on Lord Torinara's explanation of his actions.

"I could not, of course, sacrifice all those people of Kyotu to preserve an espionage network. But I figured that Hakido was the only one—he was a most secretive man—who knew of his trap for you. If I could kill him, and make it look like a skirmish, I might seal his lips forever, save the people of Kyotu, and I had full faith in your ability to survive, to reestablish a network.

"Finally, and most important, I took this action for you. You, too, are a life, and a life must be protected."

And then the great Lord Torinara had raised his arms to the sky and looked at Meiko with what she thought were tears in his eyes.

"*Kunoichi,* I salute you!"

GLOSSARY

There are some terms in this glossary that will not be found in the book. We list and explain them because we believe they will provide a better understanding of the extent of ninja training, knowledge and thought, and be useful to those who wish to continue their studies of this fascinating art.

AISHA: Ability by which a ninja manipulates a soft-hearted person.

AOSO: A form of hemp used to make a bowstring.

ARQUEBUS: Early rifle introduced to Japan by Portuguese in 1542.

ASHIKO: Spikes attached to the feet to aid in climbing.

AYIGASA: A silk-lined rush hat worn by samurai in the street.

BAJUTSU: The art of horsemanship.

BISENTO: A spear with a broad blade.

BO: A staff—approximately five feet long.

BOJUTSU: The art of using the staff.

BOKKEN (BOKUTO): A wooden sword used by samurai for training. Though usually made of hardwood, there are hollow, lighter versions. The great swordsman Musashi killed an opponent with a bokken in a duel.

BUDDHIST: Follower of the religion based on the teachings of the Buddha during the sixth and fifth centuries B.C. Disciples took vows against killing, stealing, lying, strong drink, etc. They lived an austere life in an effort to achieve Nirvana, a state of complete, blissful detachment.

BUDO: The way of the military (martial ways).

BUJUTSU (BUGEI): The fighting arts of the samurai. It includes weapons, unarmed fighting as well as other martial skills such as horsemanship.

BUSHI: Another word for samurai (knight).

BUSHIDO: The way of the samurai, the way of the bushi. This warrior's code governed the life and death of the samurai.

BUTOSAN KEMPO: Fist-fighting style developed in China. Known there as wu-tang-shan.

CALTHROP: *See* TETSU-BISHI.

CHAKUZEN JUTSU: The art of hiding in ceilings.

CHIKAIRI JUTSU: Art of infiltrating enemy lines or fortifications.

CHIKUJO JUTSU: The art of constructing fortifications.

CHIKYU JUTSU: Method or art used by captured ninja to convince an enemy he has betrayed his own side until he has the opportunity to escape and rejoin his own people.

CHUNIN: Ninja "lieutenants"—seconds-in-command.

DAIMYO: Territorial or local lord in feudal Japan.

DAISHO: Pair of swords worn by samurai and nobles —one short, one long.

DAITO: The "big sword." There were two types of daito, the tachi and the katana.

DESHI: A student.

DO: The way. (For example: Judo—the gentle way; Budo—the military way, etc.)

DOKA: A portable heating unit carried by ninja to warm his hands and light fires.

DOKYU: A catapult.

DO-TON JUTSU: The art of hiding oneself or gear among rocks or uneven ground.

ENNYU JUTSU: Art of using deception to penetrate enemy lines.

ENTEKI: Long-distance archery.

FERUZE: Hollow staff containing chain with iron ball at its end. The other end of the chain is attached to the staff. Chain and ball can be whipped out and whirled at opponent.

FUKIDAKE: A blowgun (blowpipe) which was sometimes nine feet long.

FUKIYA: Darts used in blowgun.

FUKUMI-BARI: Tiny darts and pins kept in the mouth to blow into enemy eyes.

FUKURO-GAESHI ZEN JUTSU: The art of infiltrating enemy lines to bring about dissension between a lord and his relatives.

FUTOKORO-TEPPO: Bronze pistols.

GEINYU JUTSU: The art of infiltrating enemy lines and causing havoc by setting fires.

GEKIGAN-JUTSU: The art of using a ball and chain.

GENIN: Ninja agents—the spies and saboteurs.

GENKOTSU: The assaulting of vital points.

GERI: Kick.

GETA: High wooden clogs worn during inclement weather and used by ninja for walking on ice to develop balance and the ability to walk silently.

GISHO-GIIN JUTSU: The art of forgery.

GO JO: Five "feelings" in people: vanity, cowardice, soft-heartedness, hot temper, laziness.

GOSHIN-JUTSU: The art of self-defense.

GO YOKU: Five basic desires: hunger, sex, pride, pleasure and greed.

GUNBAI: Iron or wooden war fan carried by samurai officers to signify rank, to signal with or to use as a weapon.

GYAKUTE: Hand-twist to bring opponent to ground.

GYOKURO: A poison preparation of brewed green tea mixed with miso-shiru (soybean paste).

HACHIMAKI (TENUGUI): Towel wrapped around head to serve as padding under a warrior's helmet.

HACHIMAN: Shinto God of War.

HAKAMA: Floor-length, divided and pleated skirt often worn over kimono or other garment.

HANSHI: Master.

HARA-KIRI (SEPPUKU): Ritual suicide—disembowelment by cutting open abdomen with short sword or dagger.

HATTORI CLAN: Ninja family led by Hanzo Hattori.

HAYAGAKE-JUTSU: Art of developing greater speed in walking and running.

HENGEN-KASHI JUTSU: Study and knowledge of disguises.

HENSU JUTSU: The art of blending into the fabric of a community.

HIKMEYA (HIKI-YA): Arrow with whistling head used for signaling.

HIRA KAMAE: Natural posture—hands on hips, feet apart.

HOJO-JUTSU: The art of binding an enemy with rope.

HOJUTSU: The art of using firearms.

HOKO: Polearm consisting of long straight head with side blade at right angles.

HYUNKU: Small bowl.

IAI: Fast sword draw.

IAIJUTSU: The art of drawing a sword.

INCHIMONJI KAMAE: Defensive posture—leading hand open.

INPO: The art of hiding.

INU-OI: Samurai sport of shooting dogs from horseback with bow and arrow.

ISSHIN-RYU: Okinawan karate known for its powerful, lightning-fast blows.

JIRAI: Land mines.

JIGAI: Ritual suicide by a woman accomplished by slitting or puncturing the artery of the throat.

JO: A short staff (stick).

JOEI-ON JUTSU: The art of moving soundlessly to penetrate an enemy camp.

JONIN: Ninja leader.

JOJUTSU: The art of the stick.

JUMOMJI KAMAE: Offensive posture.

JUNAN TAISO: Ninja exercising similar to yoga.

KABUTO: A helmet worn by samurai as part of their armor.

KAJIMI: A school of kyudo (archery).

KAMA: A sickle or scythe developed as a weapon.

KAMAE: Posture (*See* HIRA KAMAE, INCHIMONJI KAMAE, JUMONJI KAMAE).

KAMEIKADA: Rafts made of bamboo or wood set on sealed, watertight jars to provide flotation.

KARUMI-JUTSU: The art of lightening oneself for jumping, climbing, dodging.

KATANA: Long sword.

KENJUTSU: Swordsmanship.

KI: Internal or intrinsic energy or force.

KIAI: The martial shout. The kiai is used to increase power, clear the mind, build confidence in the attacker and frighten an opponent.

KISHA: Taking advantage of an enemy's desire to bribe a ninja.

KOGAI: A skewerlike tool carried in the scabbard of a short sword. Used as a comb, an eating utensil or as a "calling card" by being left in the ear of a slain enemy.

KOPPO: Bone-breaking techniques.

KOSHIRAE: All parts of the sword other than the blade.

KOTO-RYU: A school that teaches Koppo techniques.

KOZUKA (KODZUKA): Small throwing-knife carried in the pocket or in the scabbard of a sword.

KOZUTSU: Wooden guns that fire metal balls.

KUJI-KIRI: Achieving spiritual perfection.

KUNAI: A tool for boring holes.

KUNASHI: A digging tool.

KUNOICHI: Female ninja agents.

KUSARIGAMA: A sickle attached to a long chain that has a weight at the end. The weighted chain would be thrown to ensnare a victim or his weapon; the sickle then would be used to disable or kill him.

KYOBAKO-FUNE: A collapsible craft for use on water that is shaped like a wooden chest.

KYOJUTSU TEN KAN HO: The art of making an enemy think you're going to do one thing and then doing something else.

KYOKETSU-SHOGEI: A cord with a metal ring at the end and a knife at the other. Another weapon that can be used to ensnare and kill.

KYONEN JUTSU: The art of exploiting the fear of an enemy.

KYUDO: The art of the bow (archery).

MA-AI: The space between opponents—an important factor in a fight. The exact space was decided by the weapons used.

MANRIKI GUSARI: A chain, approximately three feet long, weighted at both ends.

MANTRA: Vocalization of a formula believed to embody the divinity invoked and possess magical power.

MI: The blade of a knife or sword.

MIKKYO: Ancient Japanese religious philosophy— "secret knowledge."

MIZUGUMO: A device used to walk on water ("water spider"). Four pieces of wood were attached together to form a crude ring. A piece of wood was placed in the center of the ring and attached to it by three ropes. The ninja would step on the center board of two of these rings and "slide" over the water. This instrument, for obvious reasons, failed more often than it worked.

MIZUKAKI: Swimming device worn on feet much like present-day swim fins.

MOKU-TON JUTSU: The art of hiding in grass, trees or foliage.

MUDRA: A code of hand positions signifying each of the nine steps to perfection.

MUGEI-MUMEI JUTSU: The art of being anonymous— an important factor in ninja training.

MUSHA-SHUGYOSHA: Swordsmen who traveled around Japan in search of additional training. They would challenge area champions to learn new techniques and improve their skills.

NAGAMAKI: A polearm consisting of a long, nearly straight blade with its tang inserted in a short staff.

NAGINATA: The "sword spear." A short (two-foot) steel blade whose tang is inserted into a long (six-foot) wooden shaft. At one time it rivaled the sword in popularity.

NAWANUKE JUTSU: The art of escaping from bondage by dislocating one's joints.

NEKADE: Fur sheaths with real animal claws worn on the hands.

NINJUTSU: The art of stealth.

NITO RYU: The two-sword school that taught techniques with the long sword held in the right hand, the short in the left.

NUKI-ASHI: Stealthy step.

NYUKYO JUTSU: The art of developing timing to infiltrate an enemy camp.

OBI: Sash or belt.

OSAKU: Lockpick.

O-YUMI: A twelve-foot crossbow or catapult.

RONIN: A samurai with no lord to serve.

RYAKUHON JUTSU: The art of penetrating enemy territory pretending to be a friend.

RYOHAN JUTSU: The art of kidnapping an important personage and holding him as hostage.

RYU: A school or style of a martial art.

SASUMATA JUTSU: The art of using a forked staff to hold a man.

SENJO JUTSU: The art of troop deployment.

SENSEI: Teacher.

SEPPUKU: See HARA-KIRI. *Seppuku* is a more polite term.

SHIBA GAKURE JUTSU: The art of hiding in various environments, such as among bales, straw, wood, etc.

SHIHAN: Master teacher.

SHIKOMI ZUE: A swordcane used by the blind and by

the ninja when he was disguised as a blind man.

SHIKORO: A primitive hacksaw.

SHINDO MUSO RYU: A school employing the jo (short stick) as its main weapon.

SHINKEN-SHOBU: A fight to the death, especially with swords.

SHINOBI BUNE: Small boats used to transport a single man.

SHINOBI SHOZOKO: The uniform worn by ninja.

SHINOBI-ZUE: A hollow ninja staff that conceals a chain weighted at the unattached end.

SHOGUN: "Generalissimo"—the military dictator.

SHUKO: A metal band that slips over the hand and has four spikes protruding from the palm side.

SHURIKEN: Small, pointed metal missiles ("stars") concealed easily in the obi or in a small pouch and thrown to divert, wound or kill an enemy (not mainly a killing weapon).

SHUTO: Knife-hand strike (open-hand).

SODEGARMI-JUTSU: The art of ensnaring a victim with a barbed pole.

SOJUTSU: The art of the spear.

SUIEI-JUTSU: The art of swimming and fighting in or under water.

SUIJOHOKO-JUTSU: The art of crossing water.

SUYARI: A straight spear with a long blade.

TABI: Socks with a separate space for the big toe.

TACHI: A type of long sword usually well-ornamented and worn with armor or for ceremonial occasions.

TAIJUTSU: The art of the ninja of Dr. Hatsumi's Togakure Ryu system.

TANEGASHIMAN: Early gun brought to Japan by Portuguese (arquebus).

TANUKI GAKURE JUTSU: The art of climbing a tree like an animal.

TATAMI: A straw mat.

TEKAGI: A hook worn on the hand like a shuko, used for climbing or as a weapon.

TESSEN-JUTSU: The art of using the iron hand fan.

TETSU-BISHI: Small, four-pointed metal weapon designed so that when thrown or placed on the ground, one point will always point up to stop or hinder pursuers. Points were sometimes coated with poison.

TETSUBO-JUTSU: The art of using a long iron bar.

TOGAKURE RYU: The thirty-fourth–generation ninja system directed by Dr. Masaaki Hatsumi. Founded in approximately 1550.

TONKI: Small metal weapons like shuriken, darts, tetsu-bishi, etc.

TONPO: Methods of escape.

TORIDE: An early grappling art later incorporated into jujutsu.

TSUBA: A sword guard located between the blade and grip.

TSUBA-GIRI: A tool much like a crowbar for opening locked doors.

TSUKA: The hilt of a sword or knife.

TSUKI: Punch with a ninja fist.

TSURA: Bowstring.

UKIDARA: Large pots into which ninja would step to paddle over water.

YAMABUSHI: A mountain warrior priest.

YARI: A spear primarily used as a thrusting weapon.

YAWARA: A five- or six-inch stick, made of wood, metal or other hard substances and held in the closed hand (fist). Protruding ends can be used to apply pressure on nerves or to strike vital parts of an enemy.

YAZUTSU: A quiver for arrows—usually worn by horseman.

YOKO-ARUKI: Walking sideways.

YOROI-TOSHI: An armor-piercing dagger shaped like a spike.

YUBI: An attack with the thumb to an enemy's kidney.

YUMI: A six- or eight-foot bow, the longest in the world.

ZAGARASHI-YAKU: A poison made from fruits like the green plum or peach.

ZEN: A form of Buddhism brought to Japan in the twelfth century that teaches life is transitory and death is inevitable. It was the religion of the samurai.

BIBLIOGRAPHY

Adams, Andrew. *Ninja: The Invisible Assassins*. Burbank, Calif.: Ohara Publications, Inc., 1973.

Doyle, Chuck. "The Beautiful, Brutal Art of Ninjutsu." *Masters of Self-Defense* (February 1975), pp. 42–49.

Draeger, Donn. *Ninjutsu, The Art of Invisibility*. Phoenix, Ariz.: Phoenix Books, 1977.

Duncan, Ron. "An Introduction to Weapons." *Official Karate Annual* (Fall 1974), pp. 8–11.

Durant, Will. *The Story of Civilization: Part 1, Our Oriental Heritage*. New York: Simon and Schuster, 1954.

Gard, Richard A. (Edited by). *Buddhism*. New York: George Braziller, Inc., 1962.

Hackin, J. and others. *Asiatic Mythology*. New York: Crescent Books, A Division of Crown Publishers, Inc. (N.D.).

Hayes, Stephen K. "The Deadly Ninja Are Alive and Well in Japan!" *Official Karate*, vol. 11, no. 82 (April 1979), pp. 18–20.

Hayes, Stephen K. "Extended Realities of the Ninja." *Black Belt '80* (Annual), pp. 22–27, 78–81.

Hayes, Stephen K. *The Ninja and Their Secret Fighting Art*. New York: Charles E. Tuttle Co., 1981.

Hayes, Stephen K. "Ninja Combat Method." Atlanta, Ga.: Beaver Products, 1975.

Hayes, Stephen K. "The Ninja Mind." *Black Belt* (January 1980), pp. 32–39.

Hayes, Stephen K. *Ninja: Spirit of the Shadow Warrior*. Los Angeles, Calif.: Ohara Publications, 1980.

Hayes, Stephen K. *Shadows of Iga* (An Association of Ninjutsu Scholars and Enthusiasts), Vol. 4, Issue 5 (September/October 1980).

Hosey, Timothy. "Samurai Women: Masters of Broom and Sword." *Black Belt* (December 1980), pp. 43–48.

Kerr, Lesley-Anne. "Dance of Death: A Story Whose Time Has Come." *Fighting Stars* (June 1980), pp. 28–33.

Marden, Luis. "Bamboo, the Giant Grass." *National Geographic,* vol. 158, No. 4 (October 1980), pp. 502–529.

Mashiro, N., Ph.D. *Black Medicine: The Dark Art of Death.* Boulder, Colorado: Paladin Press, 1978.

McLoughlin, Chris. "Ninjutsu: A New Look at the Art of Assassins." *Official Karate Annual* (Winter 1977–78), pp. 6–11.

McLoughlin, Chris. "Ninja." *Warriors,* No. 7 (December 1980), pp. 26–29, 46, 52–53.

Musashi, Miyamoto. *A Book of Five Rings* (translated by Victor Harris). Woodstock, New York: The Overlook Press, 1974.

Oyama, Masutatsu. *This Is Karate.* New York, Tokyo, Rutland, Vt.: Japan Publications Trading Co., 1965.

Perrin, Noel. *Giving Up the Gun: Japan's Reversion to the Sword, 1543–1879.* Boulder, Colorado: Shambhala Publications, Inc., 1979.

Reischauer, Edwin O. *Japan—The Story of a Nation.* New York: Alfred A. Knopf, Inc., 1970.

Reischauer, Edwin O. *The Japanese.* Cambridge, Mass.: The Belknap Press of Harvard University Press, 1977.

Sollier, Andres and Györbiró Zsolt. *Japanese Archery —Zen in Action.* New York: John Weather Hill, Inc., 1969.

Winderbaum, Larry. *The Martial Arts Encyclopedia.* Washington, D.C.: Inscape Corp., 1977.

ABOUT THE AUTHORS

AL WEISS has been actively involved in the martial arts for over twenty years. In addition to his practical martial arts experience, he has produced a number of publications dealing with the Oriental fighting arts. In 1962, he published *Karate,* the first popular book on the subject. Others followed, including *Tai Chi* and *Kung-Fu Wu-Su,* by Chinese Master Alan Lee.

In 1968, he founded *Official Karate* magazine, the first American periodical devoted to exclusive coverage of karate. Mr. Weiss continues to serve as editor and creative head of *Official Karate,* which has grown in popularity throughout the years and is now distributed in over fifty countries.

He is also the editor of *Warriors* magazine, which he began for Ideal Publications two years ago. He is listed in *Who's Who in the Martial Arts* and has received many awards from martial arts organizations here and abroad.

Mr. Weiss began his karate training in the shotokan style under sensei John Kuhl. A few years later, they both switched to the more fluid goju style, in which Al Weiss presently holds a fifth degree black belt.

Mr. Weiss has produced a number of martial arts tournaments throughout the country, as well as a full-contact program in Puerto Rico in 1974. He also serves as a referee and judge at tournaments throughout the United States and helped create the United States East Coast Karate Alliance.

TOM PHILBIN has been a free-lance writer for about eight years, but has been writing for well over twenty. He's done a wide variety of books on such diverse subjects as home improvements and repair, money saving, sharks, and Hollywood celebrities. He's also written for the TV show "Hawaii Five-O" and has a first novel, *The Yearbook Killer,* coming out this year.

Mr. Philbin says his interest in ninja developed in the Bronx, where he was raised. "Knowledge of arson, espionage, empty-hand combat, weaponry and assassination were useful there," he says. "We lived in a pretty rough neighborhood."

Tom lives on Long Island with his wife and three teenagers—two girls and a boy. "If any one of them tries to assassinate me," he says, "I'll be ready."